ALSO BY Amie Ryan

Green Shoes Mean I Love You
Marilyn: Loved By You

Starfish on Thursday

ESSAYS

AMIE RYAN

JavaTown
PRESS

For information, JavaTown Press, 1425 Broadway #23499, Seattle, WA. 98122

Acknowledgment is made to the following, in which stories in the collection first appeared, some in slightly different form: Medium.com: "Buyin' Guns Naked," "Dibs on Whales," "The Good School"; SMITH The Moment: "Tommy."

ISBN-10: 1502748290
ISBN-13: 978-1502748294

Library of Congress Control Number 2016909775

www.amieryan.com

Cover design and illustration by Dane Egenes

FROM ONE SEATTLE DAUGHTER TO ANOTHER

To Frances Bean Cobain

CONTENTS

ACKNOWLEDGMENTS

Thank you to Steve Murray and Damon Lockwood for their steadfast support of my work; to Dane Egenes for once again creating a wonderful bookcover; to my son, for being understanding about having a mother who writes—and often speaks—without a censor and who has learned to like this about me. I love you Nick. xoxo

Note to the reader:

I am often asked if the stories I write are true. With the exception of three satirical pieces in this collection (all in the form of letters), the stories are true but in some cases I have changed names, physical descriptions and other personal identifiers in order to protect the privacy of the people in these stories. The quotes used in the stories, however, are exact.

Starfish on Thursday

GREETINGS FROM THE DARK SIDE

I share this story out of a love for humanity, yes I mean YOU, you and yours, and may this be a cautionary tale about the danger of greeting cards.

I have an aunt, whom I will call Aunt Dottie. Dottie and I had an unspoken agreement by which we were related on paper but never saw each other. The last time I'd seen her was at my high school graduation, over 25 years ago. Since that time she had continued to send me a small gift on my birthday and at Christmas and each time I'd send her a Thank You card, or thank you letter of some kind and every Christmas I'd send her a card.

Now true, as an adult you might think I could reciprocate by sending HER gifts in return but for whatever reason, I never started doing that and so not doing that became the habit. In the world of my aunt and I, I am effectively nine years old.

She actually lives less than 25 minutes away so you might imagine we'd see each other but neither of us has ever had the idea to mention this. What can I tell you, some families are warmer than others.

In any case, three years ago my Aunt Dottie ticked me off big time. I never minded sending a Thank You card but then again, it was my idea to send one, unprompted, within 4-5 days of getting a gift. There was no stress involved; it felt like an honest, friendly thing. And so I put a thank you in the mail for Dottie, which she was going to receive four days after I got her gift. Whatever it says about my upbringing, I still maintain this was a speedy enough thank you.

But the same day I mailed out her thank you, Dottie changed the game.

After work I came home to find a message on my answering machine. I still had a land line and my answering machine played the messages out loud, into the room. My aunt was in her car, talking on her cell phone, sounding falsely concerned but mostly griping about if I had received her gift (i.e. why had she not gotten a thank you yet). She went on about this for a minute or two and then said goodbye and believed she had hung up her phone.

She hadn't. And so my answering machine continued to record her conversation with my uncle and I heard my aunt's tone change instantly as she described me as an "ungrateful bitch" who was late in sending the thank you. I could hear my uncle making feeble attempts to defend me which resulted in him getting yelled at as well. Several minutes of this recording went on, which although accidental, still changed my feelings for my aunt.

Actually, when I went to send her a thank you I discovered I had no stationery, no blank notecards of any kind, not even notebook paper and envelopes and I was tapped out due to the holiday. I did have several extra Christmas cards though, so I decided to be amusing and practical at the same time and sent her a second card and inside the card I began: I'm sorry I don't have any thank you cards so I guess you're getting a second Christmas card to say I continue to send you Christmas wishes and to thank you for the beautiful bracelet.

I included two or three paragraphs, warmly thanking her for her thoughtfulness. The exact same paragraphs I would have included in a thank you card or letter. In my mind, this counted as a thank you.

She received this on Thursday. On Saturday I received a manila envelope from her which contained three blank Thank You cards with envelopes and a package of stamps and numerous address labels for my aunt. There was no note of explanation but then again, no note was needed.

I'm a female. I speak fluent female bitchery. This was her way of saying my thank you had NOT been accepted and instructing me how to do it properly and without any excuses of not having her address or postage.

At this point, men and women are reading this story differently. The men, I imagine, are thinking, hmm that's pretty weird. The women hear an entirely different story. The women right now are saying, Oh No She Didn't. Because you see women do this all the time. Women fire opening shots sometimes right over the heads of men who remain oblivious. To you men, all I can say is: male fights last seven minutes. Female fights last DECADES.

You see, we have a hard drive. Everything goes on the hard drive. Most especially in regard to other women, who are held to a higher standard because we know THEY also have the hard drive. True, we keep track of male bad behavior, but it's in its own category.

Whether fair or unfair, be glad you're in a different category. True it may mean we're factoring in that you're monkeys; that you are less accountable, less thoughtful by nature, less able to empathize. Less less less. Don't take that bad, take that good. It means we continue to deal with you. It means you live to try again another day.

I can hear some men sounding sarcastic at this moment, saying "Well gee, thank you," and you should thank us. Because a female with a grudge is a terrifying thing. Seriously, be so glad for that Y chromosome pal, because without it, your world would be a different place.

Go find a female who has a beef with another female. Now ask her when the ORIGINAL problem started. Tell yourself to keep a straight face. You'll probably learn that the ORIGINAL slight happened years and years ago and involved either a funny tone of voice or a kind of funny look on someone's face. Something a male would have never registered to begin with.

Often the comment that begins female wars is this: Hmm. You read that correctly. One woman will say something and the other one will respond by simply saying Hmm. But it's all in the tone. When a bitchy tone is applied to Hmm it changes the meaning and becomes F*** You.

Every woman reading this is nodding her head right at this moment.

You see women, for whatever reason, are less likely to come right out with what they mean because then they'd be held accountable for that opinion, or thought of differently because they said it straight out. We're taught, from childhood on, that this is how you express F*** You. You say Hmm. In that tone. It is instantly recognizable to every female over the age of about eight years old. You hear that Hmm, you duck for cover because a war just started.

Every female in the room will immediately make the same translation. There is no confusion. On their own hard drives they'll be marking the time and day this particular war began because they know they'll be sharing the information later, with other females.

If there are men in the room they will be completely clueless anything has occurred. They'll ask what time the game starts or will stir their coffee.

Usually the person who just responded Hmm will then say some neutral sounding sentence, but one which will jibe with her Hmm. Then the first woman will often respond with Hmm and a crossing of the legs. This is upping the ante and is translated into Oh Yeah Well F*** You and F*** Your MOTHER.

Later on the women may try to get support from the men, will remind them of how that woman said Hmm and the men will be bewildered: "What? She said Hmm? How is that bad?" Trying to explain will be useless. The men, if they cannot offer support, will usually tread gently because they at least understand that something of importance took place and they don't want to be punished.

I'm in my midforties and have several female friends who are still immediately, actively pissed about verbal slights from other females they received prior to the sixth grade.

I digress. My point is, when I received the manilla envelope full of the silent scolding and the unspoken demand for a SECOND thank you, and this time a proper one, I put my foot down. I had sent her a genuine thank you. Whether on a Christmas card or Thank You card or scribbled on the back of a racing form, a heartfelt thank you is a thank you and that's what is supposed to matter.

I refused to send her a second thank you or to acknowledge that she had send the thank you cards to me. Take that. On the hard drive. Merry damn Christmas.

So this incident passed and then for two years we were on the same program, with one major difference. Each time I received anything from my aunt I was instantly filled with stress, worried I wouldn't get the thank you in the mail quickly enough. Before I could even finish unwrapping the gift I was mentally planning when I needed to get her thank you in the mail. This made me dread hearing from her and made me actively dislike even the thought of her.

Last year she changed things up. Out of nowhere she sent me a Thanksgiving card.

Just a word here, I do not send Thanksgiving cards. I think they're an iffy thing and not something I want to become associated with. I tend to think people who send them are Martha Stewart showoffs with too much time on their hands who are using a holiday as an occasion to make the rest of us feel uncivilized. I don't want to even begin to be the kind of person who sends out Thanksgiving cards because once you start, you've set a precedent and have to send them forever and also because if I sent them I'd be making the recipients feel horrible.

Not to mention, she lives 25 minutes away and could have actually INVITED me to Thanksgiving DINNER instead of sending me a card. Really the card seemed to be a way of saying: Hi, we aren't inviting you to Thanksgiving, hope someone gives you turkey.

Please don't defend the Thanksgiving cards. Truly, if there's a situation where you are communicating with a loved one who would be welcome at your table but for urgent reasons cannot be there (SUCH AS FIGHTING IN A WAR OVERSEAS) then you send your greetings in a letter. Taking the time to purchase a Thanksgiving card to mail prior to the holiday means you took the time to think about how you aren't inviting them to eat dinner with you and you wanted to be sure to let them know. It's the most backhanded greeting card of all time.

But because it came from my aunt, I was gripped with anxiety about whether I needed to send a thank you for the Thanksgiving card. Running to the store to purchase my own Thanksgiving card was not an option, as I had already taken a moral stand against it (see earlier paragraph). Because I wanted to end my own stress as quickly as possible, I gave in and sent her a proper Thank You card, which contained several handwritten paragraphs thanking her for the Thanksgiving card. Sometimes you do what you have to do.

Then she sent me a Thank You card for my Thank You card.

This made me do two things: curse out loud, standing at my mailbox, and wonder if I was supposed to now send her a thank you for her thank you for my thank you for the original unwanted and disliked and resented Thanksgiving card.

Which, by the way, should not exist.

I sent no further messages in the mail. Someone needs to draw the line on the overthanking. Which in this case wasn't even overthanking or genuine thanking, it was pure fear and resentment.

Yesterday afternoon I received a birthday gift from my aunt. Stationery with stamps. I understood. I immediately dashed her off a thank you letter. It's going out in today's mail. Not that I felt any happiness doing so but only because I had been scolded NO NO BAD DOG and trained to do so. Because Thank You cards are now flaming arrows. Because of the hard drive. Because we're women and we're family.

TOMMY

My older sister is not a warm person. Jessie hates the world and wants the world to know. Why that is or when it began, we never knew. Smile at her and you'll get a glare. Say anything nice and she'll ask you what the hell you mean by that. Just exist and she'll probably want to hit you. My mother used to sum it up by saying: it's just her way.

And then, when she was 24, my sister made an exception and liked something: her cat, Tommy, a black and white kitten named for a rock opera. You might imagine we found it nice to hear her speaking softly, to see anything actually bringing a smile to her face. But it wasn't nice. On my sister, it just looked wrong. And since it proved she was capable of kindness, it only showed she was being intentionally mean all the rest of the time.

And so we all carried a little resentment toward the kitten. Not that he bothered anyone. In fact Tommy was as dull as dust while he was alive but after he died he made things very exciting at our house, as you will see.

We had had numerous pets and always felt bad when one of them died but part of the process always involved getting the deceased pet out of there ASAP. For some reason, when my parents discovered Tommy dead in the garage they decided to leave him there until my sister could see him, if she chose.

This horrified me and I told them so. And was voted down.

And so, late that night, my sister came home and did indeed want to go see Tommy. She stayed in the garage for three hours as my parents and I exchanged looks and wondered what she was doing in there. When my sister came back into the house my mother asked her, gently, if it was okay if we "took care" of Tommy and my sister became hysterical.

"DON'T YOU DARE MOVE MY CAT!" she yelled.

And so they didn't.

We lived in Kirkland, a suburb of Seattle, and you've probably heard it rains in Seattle all the time. It doesn't. Sometimes, in the summer, the weather can go up into the 90s and beyond. Sadly for us, Tommy died in the middle of a weirdly hot July. Day One of the dead kitten became Day Two and it was 88 degrees by 10am. My father kept the garage doors shut because, as he confided to my mother and I, "otherwise the neighborhood dogs will smell that cat and drag him all over and we'll have little busted pieces of Tommy all up and down the street."

Day Two became Day Three (90 degrees) and then Day Four (92) and the garage became a scary place. My sister was spending over seven hours a day out there. We didn't know what she was doing and were afraid to guess. When she was inside the house she would wander up and down the hallway, wailing, sometimes in gibberish and sometimes almost coherently. She wailed things to God. She wailed things to Tommy. Sometimes it was unclear which one she was speaking to.

"He's a pinball wizard," my sister told my mother.

"Yes," my mother agreed, "yes."

The family began to organize shifts to be sure one of us was at home with Jessie at all times. Each time my parents said they worried she'd do something crazy, they corrected themselves: "crazier."

Day Five was a recordbreaker (95 degrees), and my sister stopped being aware of things going on around her. She might have still been vaguely aware where she was, we weren't quite sure, but she was disconnected, and didn't seem to see or hear anything going on around her. This was frightening but also convenient as we could now discuss her behavior while standing right next to her without her noticing a thing.

My sensitive parents had stopped being sensitive. "What if I need a wrench or something?" said my dad. "Maybe we need to put her in a place," said my mom, using her euphemism for mental hospital. "I don't know," said my dad, "but we need to do something." It was a serious situation: they had lost access to their garage.

It was my suggestion we take advantage of my sister's altered state by waiting until she was asleep and then just removing Tommy and telling her God had taken Tommy to Heaven. I was voted down.

And then in the middle of Day Six (91 degrees) my sister agreed we could move Tommy. We could put him in a box and put the box in the trunk of my mother's car, but that was it. We couldn't move the box out of the trunk until my sister gave further instructions.

The rest of us all had the same thought at the same time: we needed to call David. David was in the third grade and lived next door. For a long time we all found him creepy until we discovered we could ask him to remove any dead offerings our cats left on the welcome mat. Birds, mice, squirrels, you name it, one phone call and David would say "Sure!" and come running over, happy to do the deed for a dollar.

And so we called him and he said "Sure!" and my mother gave him instructions. Two minutes later he came to the front door and reported the cat was in the box but that he couldn't get the lid of the box to fit. This was too much dead cat conversation for my mother so she told him that was OK and thanked him and sent him home with two dollars, since this was a big job.

My dad, who had served in the military and liked to remind us how tough this made him, went into the garage to fix the box problem and swiftly ran back into the house, gagging. On his second attempt he was able to fit the lid on the box but confided to me later this was easier said than done.

"Well the thing is, after six days, there's rigor mortis," began my father, under his breath. He looked carefully to the left and right to be sure my sister wasn't around to overhear his words. "I couldn't fit the lid on. I had to bend him and break him." We both burst out laughing and then immediately stated "It's not funny, it's really not funny," which, as you know, must be said following clearly inappropriate laughing, to undo the bad karma.

So Tommy, dead cooked bent and broken, went into the box and the box went into the trunk of my mother's Cadillac. She said it was like transporting "some guy whacked by the mob."

My dad bleached and bleached the garage floor. My sister seemed to come back a little at a time. "Thank God we have the garage back," said my mother, and then, almost as an afterthought, "and thank God your sister is getting back to normal."

Tommy rode around in the trunk for two days and then my sister let my mother take him to the vet. He was diagnosed with feline leukemia, cremated, and put into an urn, which my sister kept on her dresser. Every day she'd talk to Tommy and every day we'd pretend to not hear her doing this.

But if you asked my sister how she was, she'd snarl "Go to hell!" and that's how we knew she was back to her old self: despising the world, which was her way.

THE FISH THROWN BACK

I used to hope I'd meet The One. Years of dating weirdos cured me of this notion as I came to fear each of them might indeed be The One and I'd be saddled with him until the day I died. Thus I came to embrace my single status, being thankful that any guys I dated were just on loan and that no paperwork had been signed. My friend Steve refers to my dating technique as Catch and Release.

Consider the following: the one who complained "Why do you always have to be thinking? Why can't you just sit there and not think?" He then specifically compared me to the Scarecrow in The

Wizard Of Oz, which temporarily led to a minor side argument about whether he meant pre-brain or post-brain. He clarified it was when the Scarecrow was singing about how if he got a brain he'd think and think some more. That, he said, was my problem. Thinking and then thinking some more. It bothered me he was dissing me for this reason and that he was using the Scarecrow to do it, as anyone can tell you the Scarecrow is the one Dorothy missed most of all.

There was the one who bragged to me about how, with his personal tragic background, he should rightfully be a serial killer. He considered this to be an asset, that he wasn't one, and this led to an argument with me insisting people are supposed to NOT be serial killers and that it isn't a bonus to NOT be one and him being irritated I didn't appreciate his non serial killer-ness, since it was the best thing about him. Then I realized it kind of was.

There was the one who worked as a mime. Yes, that kind of mime, there is only one kind. I freely admit, when I'd spot him working on a streetcorner I'd cross to the other side of the street, pretending not to know him. He claimed this behavior was unsupportive of his art. I'd claim not to have seen him and would suggest he just shout my name the next time. "You know I can't DO that!" he'd say, and I'd say "I know." He also did the mime thing whenever we had a disagreement, sometimes pretending to be me acting tough (hands on hips) or him acting sad (hands clutching what we imagine to be his breaking heart) and sometimes I would get into it and cock my finger and pretend to shoot him and then he would fall down as if I had. When this started bringing me pleasure, I decided it was time to move on.

I dated one guy for the single reason that he looked exactly like Charles Manson. Not that I have a thing for Charles Manson, I think he's a dangerous criminal and I don't find him attractive or unattractive. Still, it was terrifically amusing that I could describe my guy as looking exactly like Charles Manson and then later, when my friends would see him, they'd exclaim "My God, he really DOES look just like him!" He taught me to appreciate Led Zeppelin but soon there was a bustle in our hedgerow: he refused to hold a job. His skills seemed to be drinking coffee at Denny's, playing video games, and drawing paisley patterns with magic markers.

And so I remain single, so far not finding The One but finding many Ones that are at least good for free material after the fact. As a writer, that sometimes seems like a pretty good trade, especially when you factor in that, as a single person, I can be as bizarre as I like. This could easily translate into artistic genius or just make me a weirdo, time will tell. Still, it's nice to be able to have cake for breakfast and do laundry only when I can no longer find any clean clothing items.

Actually sometimes I just buy new clothes instead of doing laundry at all. I'm single. I can do that and answer to no one. I can talk to telemarketers in scary monster voice. I can sing Stevie Wonder songs as loudly and as badly as I feel like, anytime I wish.

One thing does make me immediately wish for a husband and that is seeing a spider and wanting someone else to kill it. For spider killing alone I would be willing to put up with a man one day a week (but not seven) but this would also have to involve me being able to push a button and have him disappear, Star Trek style, as soon as the insect was gone.

It's my secret belief that a good deal of marriages are based on the bug killing alone. In fact I think if someone clever were to design a vibrator that ALSO emitted an audible only to spiders kill sound, men would become nearly obsolete. I further believe scientists have been able to make this product for quite some time but have been unable to reveal this to the American public due to pressure from the Bible Belt. They understand: once you take away the incentive of sex and spider killing, you've got yourself a problem.

Amen, my brothers, Amen.

STARFISH ON THURSDAY

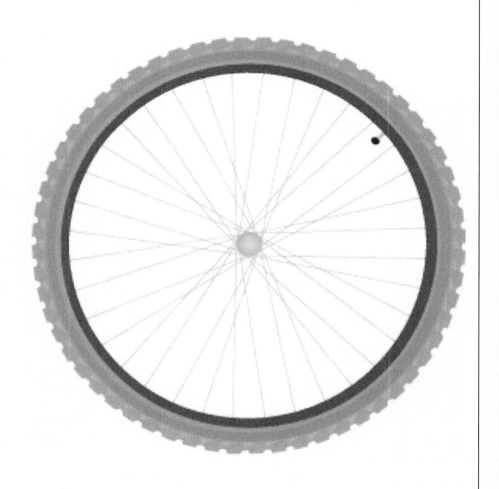

THE RUSSIANS

The most memorable feature of my parents' house wasn't part of the house at all, it was the ferociously steep hill in front of it. *A great sledding hill* you would think, as you looked at it. You'd have that thought immediately, even in the middle of summer. I don't know how high it was. I can only tell you in kid terms: it took 20 minutes to walk to the top of it and maybe 60 seconds to slide down.

From the top of this hill you could see it ended in a cross street, like the top of a capital T. Kids sledding needed to prepare, about halfway down, to make a very sharp left or right at the bottom. They couldn't go straight or they'd just end up going down our driveway and crashing into our house. It's been my experience that when faced with dangerous activities, kids are either clueless or wickedly smart. In the maybe 15 years my parents owned that house no kid ever misjudged the turn at the bottom. But because they feared that one might, my parents parked their station wagon in front of the driveway, so that if a sledder went straight, he'd run into the side of this car. My parents honestly believed this made it safer.

Whereas the hill was excellent for sledding, it was actually a pain if you were on a bicycle. Preparing to turn left or right halfway down was difficult and at the bottom you ran the risk of encountering cars in motion, a hazard not present when there was snow.

I still wonder why the Russian family couldn't see the danger. Even without being able to speak English, isn't the sight of a steep hill the same? Isn't 50+mph the same speed if you're zooming straight down a hill on a bicycle? Had they never been on bicycles before? I still don't know the answers to these questions. I also don't know why a drawing of a red cross isn't a universal symbol for first aid. And if it isn't, then what is?

But I'm jumping ahead.

I'd moved back home after my freshman year of college and was home alone, typing, when I looked out the front window and saw what looked like a family—a man and woman and a 12 year old boy—all on bicycles, flying down the hill, already way past the halfway point and going way too fast to possibly make the turn at the bottom. One second I saw them and then they were zooming down the driveway, then I lost sight of them and then I heard a terrible sounding crash as they hit our closed garage door.

I ran through the house and entered the garage that way and saw two things at once. The first was the family and their battered bikes. All three of the people were standing and looked messed up but the man and the boy seemed like they only had scraped hands and maybe skinned knees. The woman was crying in pain and holding her head with both of her hands. The second thing I noticed was the garage door was still closed but now had a feature I had believed only possible in cartoons: it had a huge, oddly shaped hole punched right through it which I immediately identified as a Wile E. Coyote hole.

There was a phone in the garage and I asked the man if they were okay, if they needed 911, and soon learned they spoke no English, only Russian. I had finished getting a D in this language only months earlier. The woman was conscious and her head wasn't bleeding but that didn't mean anything. I called 911 and told them what had happened and that none of the people could speak English. No one at 911 spoke Russian and they decided to send an ambulance so the woman could get checked at the hospital, to be on the safe side.

While I waited for the ambulance to arrive, I tried to make conversation with the man, although my Russian was limited to a handful of words I couldn't quite string together properly.

"Ye studientka universtyet. Ye studientka Russki," I told him, which (extremely) loosely translated means: I'm a university student. I am a student of Russian.

The man smiled and nodded.

"Ye galoopee," I told him. Which loosely translated means: I am a stupid.

The man and boy both laughed and the woman, still crying, got a little smile on her face.

Then the ambulance pulled up, which I thought meant I could relax and let the pros handle everything. But the three Russians became hysterical at the sight of the vehicle. As the paramedics walked toward the garage, the Russian family huddled together, all three crying and casting fearful glances at the approaching men. When the paramedics got within 12 feet the Russians began frantically waving their arms in Go Away gestures.

One of the medics had the idea that maybe their vehicle and their uniforms made them look like police. Maybe the family feared they were in trouble. This is when I thought I had come up with the genius idea OF ALL TIME to draw a red cross on a piece of paper. I pointed to the red cross, then to the paramedics. This and this.

The Russians calmed down a little but seemed to make no connection. I think they found it amusing that the Galoopee girl was drawing pictures for them.

The paramedics tried calling on their radio to find a translator and had no luck. I tried calling the local university's foreign language department, to see if anyone there spoke Russian. They did and he was on vacation until the end of the week.

Since the paramedics didn't know what else to do, they called the police department and within minutes a squad car pulled up. Because we lived in the suburbs and the police often had nothing to do, a second police car pulled up behind the first one. The sight of four uniformed policemen got the Russians going all over again. I think the actual police looked more like police than the paramedics had.

The four police officers and three paramedics all kept 12 feet away from the crying family. I decided I'd better call my mom and have her come home from work.

"I think you should come home. Three Russians on bicycles crashed through the garage door and now there's an ambulance and two cop cars here and the family's crying and won't let anyone near them," I told her.

My mom sounded strange. "Say that sentence again," she said.

I repeated it and she said she was on her way. The only thing she wanted to know was who was going to fix her garage door.

The Russians seemed glad the men were all keeping their distance. My experience with actual Russians was limited to Gorbachev, Mikhail Baryshnikov, and Boris and Natasha (who were, technically, cartoons). Thus I probably assumed all Russian people were either serious and severe looking, sexy ballet dancers, or hated Moose and Squir-rel.

Not knowing what else to do, I brought out a tray of cookies and a pitcher of iced tea for all the people in the driveway and garage. The Russians calmed down enough to smile. Apparently they understood people don't give you cookies if they're planning on arresting you.

Then, just when I'd practically become a UN Peacekeeper, my mom pulled up and was yelling before she was even fully out of the car. She wanted to know who was responsible for the garage door. The paramedics looked scared of her and also scared as they told her they didn't know.

"I don't think they're from here," one of the officers told her, "because they're speaking Russian."

"Really?" said my mother, "You must be a detective! Can I call you Columbo?" She gave him a scary smile full of shark teeth and he stayed quiet after that.

Interestingly, the Russians didn't seem upset by her at all. Maybe it was because she was wearing regular clothes and not an official looking uniform. They chuckled at her as if they were watching a comedy.

Eventually one of the Russians handed the paramedics a piece of paper with their host family's name and phone number on it and, once called, they arrived and took the Russians to the emergency room. As to my mother's question, who was going to pay for her garage door, the answer was: No One.

It turned out the Russians couldn't be held responsible, through some part of their travel visa. The officer she called Columbo tried to explain this to my mom and I knew it was a mistake. My mother was a dedicated shopper and greatly objected to the term visa being applied in any sense except credit card. I had heard her go on and on about it many times. "Why Visa?" she would ask, "Why not MasterCard or American Express? Why must they pick on Visa, can anyone TELL me why?" The only safe response was to shrug your shoulders and agree with her.

Poor Columbo. Then he had to tell her the host family also couldn't be held responsible.

"WHAT?" my mother yelled, "Well that's just GREAT, so they get to just go around crashing through people's garage doors and don't have to pay a thing?" She made it sound like something reckless teens might do for fun on weekends. "Maybe I should go to THEIR country and smash through THEIR garage door! See if they like that! But NO, if I did THAT, I'd have to pay for it! Why, it'd be an international INCIDENT! Isn't that RIGHT?" She directed this last toward Columbo.

"Ma'am, I don't know," he mumbled, clearly a little scared.

I could tell I'd have an easy week of it because, no matter what I might do, at least I wouldn't be Russian.

Columbo tried to cheer her up: "At least, from what it looks like, no one was hurt."

"My garage door?" my mother reminded him.

AMIE RYAN

DEAR GOD

Dear God,

Hi, it's Diane and I think you know why I'm writing you this letter. I need to apologize. You already know what I'm apologizing for but I'm going to say it out loud: I was a telemarketer. And I know, when You created people and made them able to speak and, technically, able to dial, You probably never intended telemarketing to exist. Much like Styrofoam, it was just something we thought was a great idea which in fact doesn't do anyone any good.

But I needed a job, God. It was the only thing available. As you know, I need to eat and groceries cost money. And I really believed them, God, I believed I was going to be helping new parents get the greatest baby photos ever, even though I'd always heard that babies are naturally photogenic and the sample photos I saw were all the most hideous pictures I'd ever seen, I still had hope.

And I didn't know the pressures I'd be under, God. I didn't know I'd be in a room with 20 other people, all of us shaking in fear as our supervisor prowled around the room, yelling threats to fire us. Well actually, You were there, You are everywhere, so You must have heard her, telling us we had to meet our quotas, telling us that without that job we'd be sleeping under a freeway, telling us that she knew within a year half of us would be holding up homemade signs, words scrawled on salvaged cardboard, WILL WORK FOR FOOD. She was scary, God. When she screamed DIAL, we dialed.

But I should have known what a pest I was becoming, not just to average people but to people trying to take care of their newborns. Calling someone six times within eight hours is excessive. Leaving someone 15 messages is excessive. I knew this and I did it anyway. And I started knowing it wasn't really on the up and up when I learned the photo company had had to change their name seven times. And You know why that was, God, it was because their company kept getting on the TV news and broadcasters kept warning viewers not to do business with them. Each time that happened they had to change their name. Not that they fooled You, but they hoped to fool all of those parents, all of them in New Jersey and Connecticut and New York, or as I thought of it, my territory. I guess everywhere is Your territory, that's what I should have remembered.

And those parents, God, the angry ones, the ones who'd done business with our company before, I believed them. When they said the hospitals had sold their information for five dollars to companies like ours, and that was why on my computer screen it had the couple's names and their kids' ages and names so I could ask how little Sarah was doing, I believed them. When they said our company was NOT the ones that took the hospital's first photos and that they in fact had NOT already paid for an in home sitting and complimentary 8x10, I believed them. When the said it was a scam so they would be tricked and hounded into buying $500 or more of horrible baby photos, I believed them.

But God, I was making good commissions by then. I know it's no excuse but it felt so good to see all that money in my hand. It felt good enough that I got better at being bad. And when I occasionally would call a new parent only to learn that our information was wrong and in fact their infant had been stillborn or died shortly after birth, when the parent would sob as they were telling me that information, I apologized and ended the call, and took a deep breath, and then dialed the next number.

And then there was the vanity, God. I liked being the top booker. I liked having the other guys hating me because I'd booked more gigs than they had. I was King Shit God, and You know how good THAT feels.

It's true, when I heard a parent hesitating on making the booking I occasionally commented, "Don't you like what your baby looks like?" It's true, to the fathers I pressed the false point that they had already paid for the service. It's true, I took advantage of the new mothers and their out of control hormones by telling them that most of the OTHER new moms had already had the photos taken by now. "Oh I can't do anything right!" so many of them would cry, and then I would help them by helping my own self, God. By helping my commission.

That's why I don't blame You for what happened next, for the way You took one tooth on each side of my mouth and made them go completely insane. You, in Your infinite wisdom (and flair for the ironic) broke my mouth so I could not speak. And after that emergency oral surgery, after the swelling went down and I could say things other than GUH UH HUH, I knew I should only use my voice for good and not evil.

And true, it still took me five more weeks to quit that job but I did, and ultimately, I learned my lesson. The gift of verbal treachery should not be used to make money. I know that now. It should only be used socially, You know, with guilt an intimidation, the way You intended. And if my spoken persuasion brings me reward, You can be sure it won't be in the form of cash, although it may come in other forms which are somewhat cash equivalent. After all, I do live in the world, God, and You know better than anyone how I like expensive gifts and also the gifts which keep on giving, such as feeling superior to others and bringing my enemies low.

It's really true, confessing IS good for the soul!

Thanks for listening,
Diane

WE DON'T COOK HERE

The first time I entered a Macy's kitchenware department I was filled with nostalgia. It looked exactly like my mother's kitchen. Shelves were filled with every kind of pricey gleaming kitchen gadget imaginable and there wasn't a sign of actual cooking anywhere.

For a while when I was younger, my mother used to cook. She'd grown up in the fifties and had been schooled in the home arts, both at home and in school. The same school that didn't really think girls would need math had written tests about ironing.

So in the beginning, and through most of the 1970s, my mother cooked and sewed. And did oil paintings. And hung wallpaper. And refinished furniture and caned chairs. But she refused to ever show my older sister or I how to do any of these things. She claimed sometimes to be too busy and sometimes that we probably wouldn't be able to catch on. As we got older her excuse was that she feared we'd break something or catch the house on fire. Personally I think she just wanted to be the only one with those skills.

Then she discovered the microwave. Soon we knew dinner was ready by hearing an electric DING and meals didn't taste quite the same. Sometimes food contained a molten center and sometimes we would guess incorrectly about what could go into the microwave. Explosions were mostly rare. We adjusted and took the same ten minutes to eat dinner and argue, the same way we had always done before, but this way my mother didn't have the inconvenience of necessary prep time before and cleanup afterward. This left her extra time to pursue her interest in watching daytime talk shows. My mother, who used to lovingly exclaim, "Oh that Marlo Thomas!" would now say "Oh that Phil Donahue!" I think she assumed he was wise right from the get go because he had married Marlo.

Although she mostly boycotted cooking, my mother continued to collect expensive cooking tools: she installed two bookcases in the kitchen pantry specifically for cookbooks and kept hundreds, arranged in an order known only to her. She requested kitchenware as gifts, specifying to the giver which make model and color to purchase. In this manner she acquired a full set of copper cookware which she hung, eye pleasingly, from the ceiling with ornate scrolled ironwork. This collection went unused and so, remained in mint condition, never needing washing, only polishing. She had crepe makers, a bread machine, a pasta maker, waffle irons, and a trio of KitchenAid mixers. Walking into the kitchen on a sunny day meant being nearly blinded by the gleam. The more gadgetry she collected, the luckier it was that she rarely cooked. There was simply no room.

Once in a while she'd still make the occasional dessert and when the other women would ask her for the recipe my mother would give it to them except with the ingredients, amounts, and cooking temperature altered. This way the other women would be bested twice: not only had they had to request my mother's recipe but even when they supposedly had it, they lacked the ability to recreate the perfection. This aspect of cooking my mother enjoyed.

Often my mother would skip the whole illusion of cooking and we'd just go out to dinner. I have nothing against this cooking method. Sometimes we'd even go to a restaurant for Thanksgiving dinner. It turns out they prepare turkey just about everywhere and we could spend the same ten minutes eating arguing and guilt tripping each other but in fancier clothes.

When I was in junior high we had one six week coed course intended to cover cooking music and sewing. The cooking segment featured two, count 'em two, items: cookies and scrambled eggs. The cookies I could never master. Several times I tried and was able to produce only a muddy lake of cookie. The scrambled eggs I got. To this day the one dish I prepare? Scrambled eggs. It's possible my high school had a cooking class of one kind or another but if so, it was nothing required and nothing I'd have sought out. Why would I seek to learn about something as useless as cooking when I could take classes I might really need someday, like drama and stained glass?

I still remember a lady I babysat for. Her name was Dorenna and when she casually mentioned I could just give her little girls a can of soup for lunch, I looked at her, bewildered. The can of soup I could recognize (the thing on the commercials and in Andy Warhol prints) but had no idea how to get the soup out of the can. I was fourteen. When I asked her how it was done, she told me I could find a can opener in the top utensil drawer. I opened this drawer, saw numerous shiny metal tools and could not identify a can opener by sight. Never once gasping in shock or pausing to comment on my idiocy, Dorenna showed me which one the can opener was. Holding it in my hand I still had no idea which part did what to open the can. And so this patient woman opened the can for me while I watched with delight. Learning you added water, learning you measured a can's worth, learning that with cream soups you added milk and yes, again a can's worth and that yes, they had planned it that way, all of these things were revelations to me. It's amazing she left me alone with her children.

By the time I was living on my own I understood I had been given a gift by my feminist soul sisters. I could choose what kind of woman I wanted to be. And the type I wanted to be had no interest in cooking. Grocery stores must have thanked God for people just like me and they were kind enough to stock their shelves with instant and precooked foods of every kind. No need to buy dozens of ingredients or spend time chopping or straining or welding or whatever it is cooks do. No need to scrub pots and pans that I still say act like they dislike being used for cooking.

And ladies and gentlemen, may I mention the invention of delis inside grocery stores. For a while I worked at one and noticed many women would come with their own Tupperware or cookware and would request we put the food items inside them so they could pretend they were homemade. These weren't exactly my soul sisters, as I took pride in my noncooking and would never have thought to hide it, but they were at least my soul cousins, and I helped them keep their secrets. In a deli you can get every possible salad, side dish and main dish. It's like a great big picnic basket, that's what I think. It also proves there must be a lot of people not cooking out there, not just me.

I understand there are people who take great pride in preparing food, for themselves or others. More power to them. I'm just not one of them. I can't understand spending more time preparing a meal than people are going to spend eating it. To me dinner is about 15 minutes worth of fuel that makes me stop feeling hungry. It doesn't mean love or devotion. It doesn't make me happy or sad.

And so I instituted the 15 minute rule. It's an excellent rule, feel free to use it yourself if you'd like. No meal can take longer than 15 minutes to prepare. That's from walking into the kitchen to sitting down to the table to eat: 15 minutes. Exceptions are made on Thanksgiving and Christmas which may take no more than 30 minutes.

Yesterday my son mentioned "those cookies you make" and I thought for a minute he had mistaken me for someone else. Turns out he was talking about the precut circles of cookie dough Pillsbury gifted us with, the ones you stick in the oven for 10 minutes. My son refers to this as my cookie recipe and really, it's the closest thing to a recipe that I have.

Some of you may be thinking 15 minutes isn't enough to make a meal but trust me, it is. What I usually do is have one pan of frozen vegetables cooking on one burner and some kind of precooked meat that I stick, frozen, on a cookie sheet and cook for 10 minutes in the oven. Potatoes or rice, I'm quite talented, I do both, and both require boiling water (which I do, myself) and mixing stuff in and stirring. With instant potatoes I get quite fancy and add a little square of butter on the top, which I mix in. So don't tell ME I don't cook.

The result of this speed cook is this: I hardly spend any time cooking and when I eat with my son I'm not exhausted or ticked off about the amount of effort I've put in. The food tastes fine to my son and he will almost certainly eat the meal in less time than the 15 minutes it took to prepare. After the meal it takes me two seconds to do the dishes because it hardly took me any to cook it in the first place.

Breakfasts? I can heat any sausage or bacon or hashed browns. But the most impressive thing I do is scramble eggs and toss in cheese and bacon and tomatoes and zucchini. I can also make crepes but none of these things violate the 15 minute rule and that's why I do them.

Dessert? Of course. But it should only involve a few minutes to serve, during which time I can easily slice a store bought cake or pie or scoop ice cream into bowls or really go expert and put together store bought shortcake and fresh berries and whipped cream. If I bake cookies, you bet, they're usually the premade dough kind and according to my son "they always come out perfect and always taste great." My other cookie recipe is opening a package of Pepperidge Farms. As a special bonus I can tell you my son will have no problems replicating the beloved tastes of his childhood. He will never get the ingredients wrong. Home will be right there waiting for him, in any grocery aisle.

I can hear you protesting. How how how will my family know I LOVE them if I don't make a flour covered martyr of myself? How can I eat dinner without proving my devotion by whacking the head off a chicken or doing unspeakable things with string and raw meat? Why, the vegetables alone! Aren't you supposed to scrub them and peel them and send them to dental school? You cannot just open up a package and stick them in boiling water.

Oh but you can. You can!

Did you know, some people make their own jam. OK now this I just do not understand. Unless a family is living in the middle of nowhere and must rely on their own crops to live off of all winter, I do not understand canning. Not for any city person who has access to Smuckers and all they provide. Do I really think I'm going to make better tasting jam than Smuckers? Come on now. That's if nothing explodes in my face as I'm making it. I already had a bad attitude about cooking. Adding in possible explosions does not increase the appeal.

My son and I do have one holiday tradition. It was not intended to be a tradition but was originally just an amusing story I told him. When I was growing up we never said Grace except at Thanksgiving and Christmas. On those occasions we would fold our hands and close our eyes and my father would say a traditional Grace, with one interesting difference. He would close the Grace by saying "...and God Bless Jimmy Hoffa."

Up until I was five years old I assumed everyone said Grace this way. I had heard about Jimmy Hoffa, someone my Teamster father referred to as his 'brother' so often that I initially thought he was my uncle. But by the time I started kindergarten I was able to retell my dad's favorite holiday story.

It's a good story. It goes like this:

In 1959 my parents got married. She was 17 and he was 18. And in the spring of 1960 when my mom delivered my older sister, the doctor told her that something was wrong with my sister's legs. To try to fix the problem my sister would need numerous surgeries and they'd have to be performed hundreds of miles away, on the other side of the state. The chance of these surgeries fixing my sister's hips and legs was quite small and the cost of even trying would be several times the amount my father could hope to earn in three years' time. By today's standards, the surgeries would cost hundreds of thousands of dollars. The doctor told my parents that my sister would walk someday but only with metal braces and canes. She might be able to swim but she would never dance or run. My mother, lying in her hospital bed, couldn't stop crying and my father felt useless. And so the next day he went to see his boss. He had started working, driving a truck, a few months before. He had heard they had some kind of medical plan. He was worried maybe he'd get fired for even asking about benefits since he hadn't been there very long.

But then he remembered my crying mother and so he did.

And after he told his boss the story the boss said "Jerry, I think you're confused. You seem to think you're my employee and I'm your boss. You're forgetting that you're a Teamster. And because you're a Teamster, I'm your brother."

When he would tell the next part, my dad would always have

tears in his eyes. He said the boss told him "..the medical care your daughter needs? Consider it done."

And then my dad would need a minute to collect himself so he could speak again. He said those words, Consider It Done, were the finest words he had ever heard in his life. My sister got those surgeries, got the physical therapy, and by age 4 was a healthy child. She runs and dances and swims and walks, never with any braces, never with a cane or even a limp.

And my dad would then describe how that kindness came to happen. That long ago before I was even born, this man Jimmy Hoffa had wanted to make life better for working men. He said that before Jimmy Hoffa, a man was only a tool, just part of the truck, and that Hoffa wanted a union so that men could be guaranteed decent lives and fair deals and so that if they needed help—like my dad had—it would be there for them and they'd never need to beg for it.

At age six I learned what a scab was. Not the on your knee kind, but the strikebreaking kind. Men who would take the jobs of the union men during a strike. And that scabs, in this way, were taking the food right off the plates of union members.

I remember numerous times when other unions, not my father's, were on strike and how we would support them by never crossing a picket line. If scabs worked there, we didn't shop there. My mother would drive three times the distance to get groceries, to be sure to shop at stores not affected by the strike. Sometimes we'd go to a store, unaware a strike was on, and as soon as we saw the picketing men and women, we got back in the car and drove somewhere else. There was no in between on this rule and Never meant Never, it didn't mean anything else. As an adult I have many faults but crossing picket lines isn't one of them.

One day I came home from school with the question: were the Teamsters involved with the Mafia? And my dad surprised me. He said he didn't know, but "possibly." And then he explained: when you get that many people and that much money, chances are there's going to be a little bit of shady business. "But do you know what I think?" my dad said, "So what if they are? It doesn't change the good they've done. And if my nose is clean, what's it to me?"

The next day I informed my second grade teacher of this answer, What's It To Me, and she never asked me anything more about the Teamster union.

My favorite part of my dad's Grace (for truly the story always told following the Grace became part of it) was when he would marvel at the dedication of the first Teamsters. I was rarely a quiet child but would fall silent listening to my dad describe how these men had been beaten in the streets to make their union. "And I mean beaten, to death, I mean they died," my dad would clarify. He said they went through all that knowing they themselves would never see the rewards of their work. They did it for all the people coming after them. "People whose faces they would never see." My dad specified they had done that for people like our family. For him and my mom and my sister and me. That Teamsters, right or wrong, good or bad, had paid for our house and the clothes on our backs and the food on our plates. "And that was pretty amazing that they did that," my dad would say. "That's why we say God Bless Jimmy Hoffa."

This story delighted my son. "Oh we need to do this," he insisted. And so, every time we say Grace, and especially at Thanksgiving and Christmas, we close the blessing with: and God Bless Jimmy Hoffa. We retell the story. The men getting beaten in the streets. The men caring about faces they would never see. The teen couple crying with their newborn daughter. My father's boss and his words: Consider It Done.

AMIE RYAN

BOMB THREAT

One habit you get into, when you have kids, is pausing before answering a question. Factoring in what they can understand, deciding, with their age, how much information they can handle. But the day my son was going through my yearbooks the first time he was 19 and so, without thinking, I threw that rule out the window and answered a question too fast.

He was flipping through the pages, laughing at the '80s hairstyles and turned up shirtcollars, asking me to point out which kids were the Preps and Wavers and Stoners, which ones were nice, which ones were jerks. He enjoyed looking at the pictures and making guesses on which were which and then finding out if his guesses were true.

Then he came to a page with a photo of three guys horsing around outside a building. The boys in the picture are all relaxed, wearing big smiles. One has his arms outstretched like a TV entertainer: TA DA for the camera. "Hey, he looks like fun...these guys look like they're standing outside...was this in gym class or something?"

And that's when I forgot to pause and instead just answered: "Hmm? Oh...no, that would've been during one of the bomb threats." I heard these words leave my mouth just a second too late to grab them back.

"WHAT?" my son was on this like a shot, so startled he at first could not form a question but instead sounded frantic, like a car alarm: "BOMB THREAT BOMB THREAT WHAT DO YOU MEAN BOMB THREAT THERE WAS A BOMB THREAT?" He stopped and stared at me, his eyes huge.

And so it was too late, I was in this conversation. I stupidly kept believing I could explain, as if words always had the power to undo other words. I told him "Well NO, it wasn't exactly a bomb threat in that there was no bomb," I heard these words and had to make a face at how badly I was already doing.

I told him we all knew it was probably just some kid who had done a prank phone call, that none of us thought there was actually a bomb. Then I had to backtrack and remind him that of course that wasn't okay, to do a prank phone call about a bomb, that's not ok, that's illegal, right?

"Right," said my kid, "So what did they do?" He looked terrified, like he was worried that the '80s me might still somehow be at risk. I cursed myself for starting this.

I told him the school would call the police and a couple of officers would come out with police dogs and they'd just take 15 minutes or so and check the school and then they'd tell us everything was OK and we'd go back inside again and finish the school day, no big deal. Times were different then. They knew it was probably just a kid playing a bad joke. Kids do dumb things, they knew that. But there was never a bomb.

I paused, hoping this was good enough. It wasn't though, because my son is a good listener. He's all about the details. He wasn't even half done with this conversation.

"Did they catch who did it?" he wanted to know.

I told him no. This was before Caller ID.

"Star 69!" my son tried. No, before that too, I told him.

"Wait a minute, you said they took 15 minutes to check the school? The two story school that held 1500 kids, and the gym and the outside buildings and the parking lots, you had two parking lots, right? You're saying they checked all the rooms and all the offices and the whole school in 15 minutes? How could they do that?"

I said I didn't know. I told him the police seemed to think it was good enough.

"And so they had you all stand outside. These guys look like they're about 10 feet away from the building. Were you all standing that close to the building?"

"Yes," I told him. It was like my school was on trial all of a sudden and I was an unhelpful witness.

"So if it HAD been a real bomb, you would have all been blown to smithereens."

I took a moment to savor the happiness that I have a son who uses the word 'smithereens'.

"Things were just different then," I tried.

"Do you mean that explosives weren't dangerous in the '80s or that in the '80s they hadn't yet discovered that explosives were dangerous?"

"OK yes of course, they were just as dangerous then as they are now, yes they knew that. I just mean no one believed anyone would actually do anything dangerous at a school. We believed it would be impossible."

I told him to look at the photo again. I reminded him that those boys didn't look scared. They were smiling for the camera. And someone else who wasn't scared as walking around taking pictures for the yearbook.

"And you said this was during ONE of the bomb threats," he added, still on track. "There was more than one?" I told him yes. He asked me how many.

I told him "Well, you might go a couple of months and not have one and then have two in one week. But it was never scary because we always knew it was someone doing a bad joke. I don't know, maybe three per quarter."

Yes, every quarter. Yes for all three years that I went to that school. Which my son informed me added up to 27 bomb threats. I hated math then.

"And they never caught who did it? Wow," said my son, "I wonder who hated you that much?"

"No one hated us," I said, suddenly defensive, "and it was probably more than one kid. It could have even been kids from our school."

This stunned him all over again.

"So the police came out each time, they came out to the same school 27 times and they never knew who made those calls and they didn't think that was a big deal?"

There was a word we hadn't said yet in this conversation and that word was Columbine.

But the conversation was there so I let it go there.

"You've heard of Columbine," I started. Columbine is a ghosty word. Said out loud, it changed the very air of the room.

My son said yes. He scooted closer to me on the couch, not seeming to notice he had done so. To be safer. Or to keep me safe. I have a good son.

I told him before Columbine no one had believed anybody would ever hurt kids at a school. No one could even imagine that. Then there had been a couple of school shootings and then Columbine and after that people understood that it could really happen.

I realized I was describing it like the olden days; this time my son was too young to remember and could only imagine. I was describing it like I was talking about saddle shoes or The Twist or Buddy Holly's plane crash. The olden days when schools were safe. And suddenly I felt guilty for all those years I'd been able to feel safe.

"And the shootings usually happen in the spring," my son added, "they call it Shooting Season." My son, who knew this term and who still had to go to public school every day with this knowledge; something I'd never had to do.

I reminded him that now schools have plans in place in case something like that happens. I told him if one of these bomb threats happened today at my old school, it would be handled very differently. Schools have plans to keep the kids safe, I repeated.

"At least they try," my son corrected me.

"Right. They try," I said.

I wished I had more I could tell him, but the very things I wanted to say might put my son at risk. I wanted to tell him to be careful with being too quick thinking of kids as Good or Bad, that maybe nothing is ever that simple. I wanted him to be able to still feel safe, to stand, like those boys, outside a school, relaxed; smiling and feeling safe, like they did in the olden days.

COOKIE PARENTS

I may be the only person on earth who gets angry at the sight of little boy scouts and girl scouts with their parents at the entrances and exits of grocery stores.

I know you've seen this before. There will be a fold out table full of the item being sold with a mother or father energetically pitching the item to shoppers. If you ask the child a question about the cookies or candy bars, the child will look confused and will frantically get the parent's attention so she can answer the question for you. Then the child, usually in uniform, can relax and go back to sitting quietly like the prop he has become.

This sight makes me angry because it's cheating, and I ought to know, having once been a Girl Scout cookie peddler myself. Not only is it cheating the system, it's cheating the kid.

Think about it. All through their childhoods kids are told not to talk to strangers when, in fact, as adults this is a skill they'll use pretty much every day. Selling these cookies door to door is their one chance to practice. In fact, they'll probably get to practice a lot of other skills too: calling grownups Sir or Ma'am, being polite even when the other person is being rude, telling someone Thank You Anyway even when they tell you No. And hearing the word No over and over and continuing to try.

In my neighborhood it was just assumed that anyone with a school age child would at some point push them into the Door to Door ranks. The unspoken rule was that you were obligated to buy your neighbor kid's item so that they would buy from your kid when the time came. Once we'd exhausted our neighborhood, we took it on the road. My mom would drive me into other neighborhoods and she'd stop the car in front of each house and watch to be sure I didn't get kidnapped as I hauled two heavy cookie filled cartons cartons up the walkway to each door.

But hear me: she stayed in the car. She wasn't the one trying to earn a badge, that was my goal and that's why she made me do the work. If I'd asked her to sell my cookies for me she would have laughed her head off and then told me not to be lazy.

So I went to each door and heard numerous variations of No. Most people said they already had enough cookies. I was seven, wearing a Brownie beanie and with my hair in two long braids. Hey, if you ask me, I was adorable, but apparently I wasn't gifted at selling.

My sister noticed that I kept returning home with the same amount of cookies I'd left with and she decided I needed to change my sales pitch. This was a rare occasion, having my big sister pay attention to me, so I listened carefully and then, the next day when my mom took me selling, I did exactly what my big sister had said.

A bored looking woman answered the door and I said "Hi, my mom says I need to sell all these cookies (sniffle) and that I can't come home (sniffle) until I sell them ALL (full sobbing here)!"

The woman bought a lot of cookies. So did the next house and the next and I learned another good skill which was Acting.

My mom was confused why I was suddenly so successful and I told her the new way my sister had told me to sell the cookies. She laughed for a long time. Then she told me it was okay but not to tell the troop leader my trick.

"Because SHE'S not the one who has to carry those heavy cartons, right?" my mom asked

"Right!" I agreed.

So yes, there was a bit of lying involved, but at least I was the one doing the lying. I think my mom agreed because if I hadn't been able to sell the cookies, she would have been stuck buying them all. In this way, the dishonesty worked out for everyone. And once I successfully sold cookies I then had to handle money and make accurate change, more skills the kids don't get when their parents do the selling for them.

And of course when I was younger the Door to Door bit didn't end with the cookies. All the kids were regulars on the sales circuit. Candy bars, Christmas decorations, magazine subscriptions. We got to know our neighbors well.

Some of my friends now take the Selling For Their Child bit one step further: the parent sells the item to friends and coworkers, taking orders, collecting the money and delivering the goods all without the child even being aware a sale has taken place.

So you parents, the ones who seem to be trying to earn Good Parent badges as you stand behind that table at the grocery store: you aren't fooling anyone. And by the way, you're 50 feet away from an entire aisle filled with lower priced cookies, many of them Pepperidge Farm. You cannot outsell them and trust me, no way are you going to outcookie them.

BUYIN' GUNS NAKED

I like to think I'm more than just an American; I'm a patriot. And that means I care about the things that make America great. And by 'things', I mean guns. As any gun owner will tell you, guns are about peace, much like greeting cards and flowers.

But lately, guns have been getting a bad rap, due to their tendency to cause death. Some people believe there are too many guns in America. As any NRA member will tell you, restricting gun sales to any particular group would be crazy. It would reduce our fine nation to a land of wimps standing around limp and unable.

Because I care about America, I've come up with a plan:

mandatory full nudity at the time of gun purchase.

I can tell this idea already has you a little excited.

Let me explain. You may think I mean full nudity is required whenever you're carrying your gun. HA HA HA no that would be silly. Where would the extra ammo go? No, my idea is full nudity only when you go in to PURCHASE your gun. Money in one hand, ID in the other, and bare ass naked.

This is an excellent idea because it's open to everyone. As any good shooter can tell you, guns are for everyone, whether they need them for hunting or self- protection or just plain feeling good. It's the right of all Americans to be able to purchase as many guns as they can afford. Guns are what America is all about.

So I say, let's restrict guns to only the people who are brave and dedicated enough to deserve them. Show your piece to get your piece, that's what I say. Let's find out just who is compensating for what.

Now I won't lie to you: this plan may involve some ridicule. Ridicule is what America's about. Guns and Ridicule. Those two things. You may have to endure some comments like "Oh there's old Snub Nose" or "Saturday Night not so Special" or "44? Looks more like a 22!" but such is the price of freedom.

You may find yourself saying: Do I really need those fries? I'm plannin' on gettin' a gun next week. In this way guns will actually be improving your health, as you will be working on your physique. You cannot let flab get between you and being an American. Not that a guy holding a gun isn't already pretty damn attractive!

The NRA is firmly behind my plan. In fact, concerned that some fine Americans might hesitate to buy guns due to body shame, the National Rifle Association has helpfully offered to provide free gym passes to all its members. In this way the NRA will be working to solve another American problem, which is obesity.

It's really true, what they say: the NRA is about Goodness.

And they see another plus to my plan. With all the gun owners standing around naked, introductions will go MUCH faster! This will lead to likeminded hookups which will in turn produce future NRA members, or as I like to call them, Bullet Babies. It's a win win.

You see, Sex is what America's all about. Guns, Ridicule, and Sex. You get those things and mister, you've got yourself some America.

RIGHT HERE ON EARTH

This story is about finding and losing. It's an apology and an explanation and most of all, a valentine. For the real Tony and Inez Walden, wherever they may be.

****

When I was five, I'd never seen a black person in real life, only on TV. Not at the store or the bank or school or anywhere. We lived in Kirkland, across the lake from Seattle, and in our suburban neighborhood, in 1973, everyone was white. I knew black people existed but from the little bit I'd been able to figure out, they all lived really far away. If any had lived nearby, I would have heard about it because it would have been news, at least dinner table news, which is where I got most of my information.

And then my mother told me the most exciting thing I'd ever heard. She said the new family moving in across the street was black. This was shocking and thrilling.

"Really?" I asked her, afraid she was just teasing.

"Really," said my mom. And this made me jump up and down.

Even though I'd never seen a black person, I was dying to do so. I had no idea there was the possibility of having a whole black FAMILY living right in our neighborhood, and directly across the street where I could see them anytime and maybe even talk to them. If you had told me Santa Claus was moving in across the street I would have been more excited, but only by a little bit. In fact, black people and Santa, they might have tied, completely even steven.

I asked her when when when and my mother, who knew me and should have known better, told me I'd just have to wait and see.

I wasn't a wait and see type of child. I couldn't wait and I needed to see immediately. And so I set up a surveillance, keeping my eyes on the still empty house, watching for any signs of the new neighbors. For the next week I watched, and by the end of the week my mind worried over many things. There was the new rule, for one. And there was the way the grownups were fighting.

And the man next door, the one from Texas, he was picking a fight with my father. It wasn't a real fight yet, not with punching. It was the right before type of fighting. I was scared he was going to hurt my father.

The way my parents were excited and scared, both at the same time. That was new. That I hadn't seen before. Which showed I was right that black people were exciting. The way my parents were picking their words carefully, with much eye contact back and forth; unsure, careful. My parents who knew everything but not this.

Also there were all kinds of new rules with these neighbors, different than the rules for white people. I had only known being good or being bad. This was a new category, being carefully good because they were black.

My mother had told me that the nicknames, the funny words they used when they talked about black people, that those words would hurt their feelings. This was confusing to me. My family had different words for Mexicans and Chinese people and Polish people and Jewish people and Italian people, for every kind of person except white people, who were just called white. If you'd asked me to, I could have written out a complete list of these names, on the spot. That's how well I knew them. That's how much I believed they were the okay, right names.

No differently than how you could call me a child or a girl or a kid and they would all mean the same thing. I thought that's how it was. That a black person was black or a nigger or a jig or a spook and it all meant the same thing and none of the words were good or bad. This was the first time I was hearing these nicknames meant anything.

I felt tricked, and so I wanted to be sure I understood this time. I asked my mother if these words were bad words. I wasn't allowed to say bad words. Usually my parents made it clear, which ones were okay, which ones would get me in trouble. But this time her answer was confusing. She said no, they weren't BAD words but that those words would make the black people FEEL bad. These words would hurt their feelings.

She said this in a slow, confused way, like it was something she'd never thought before. I asked her, if they hurt their feelings, why do we say them, and when she answered it wasn't in that confused way, it was in her regular quick way.

"Because we just do. Because everyone does," she said. And this was like she had not answered the question at all. I kept listening.

"But you shouldn't say those words around THEM," my mother specified. "Around THEM the only right word for black people is Black People. Never say any other words. And never tell them any jokes with black people in them because it would hurt their feelings and we don't want to hurt their feelings. We only say those things inside the house."

But it sounded like my parents had done something bad and that they'd taught my big sister and I to do it too. We had both told those jokes. I had felt grown up, being able to tell a joke. And now I was hearing it was bad, so I'd been bad without even knowing.

What it sounded like she was saying was to be careful so the new neighbors wouldn't know we were bad. So they'd think we were nice and like us.

And I had asked my dad and his answer had sounded slow and confused too. I wanted to be grown up. I liked understanding things. It sounded like there were secret bad words that only white people used and that they didn't turn into bad words for real unless black people were there to hear them.

I asked my dad, was that it? And he said it was hard to explain. He said if the only people telling those jokes and saying those words were white, it was easy to think they weren't bad words. It was easy to forget that. You only started thinking about how maybe they weren't such great words if there was a black person there.

My dad looked at me to be sure I was listening. "Because real people standing there can get their feelings hurt, right?" I said Right. He said we wanted the new neighbors to feel happy living here and that meant we should try to not hurt their feelings. He said I should try hard.

My dad was mad at our next door neighbor, Mr. Spears. He was from Texas and wore a cowboy hat and had gone knocking on each family's door just the day before.

I remember what happened when my dad opened the door. George Spears stood, tall anyway at 6 feet but taller still with the cowboy hat on. He took up almost the whole doorway. He looked left and right before he spoke, to be sure everyone was listening.

He looked mad. He pointed with his finger as he spoke.

"I know you heard about these niggers moving in and I want you to know we had this problem in Texas and by God, we solved it. We can't burn 'em out and we can't beat 'em out but we can freeze 'em out. They can move in here and they'll never get a single Hello out of me. I'm not going to say one word to these niggers and I advise you to do the same. I'm going to everyone's house today and I know I can count on you, neighbor."

But this last was like a question, aimed at my dad, and my dad said "I'll take it under advisement." Mr. Spears' face got red and angry and I thought he might hit my father. Between them there was the Almost Fighting thing happening, the thing with the faces and voices. I was scared. They exchanged goodbyes and my dad closed the door.

That night I asked my dad about it. I said "Mr. Spears says he won't even talk to the new people."

STARFISH ON THURSDAY

And my dad told me, "Our last name isn't Spears."

For the next few days I turned this information over in my mind. There were secret bad words that only white people said, which was okay with the white people but not okay with black people. It sounded like all white people knew this and understood it. I wanted to be grown up. I tried to understand. I was worried. It was a lot to remember and it only kind of made sense.

But then I saw cars in the driveway of the new house and felt more excited and curious than worried. With other new neighbors, the kid drill was the same: I'd go over, introduce myself, tell them where I lived and ask them if they had kids my age who would like to play. I asked my mom if it worked the same with black neighbors.

She answered with that same confused, careful way, "I guess so."

I wonder how my mom felt, watching me go, wondering what her five year old loudspeaker might say.

I remember trying to smooth my hair down before I rang their doorbell. I spent most of my time running around and my hair was frequently a mess, which was how I liked it. You couldn't run and climb trees and have neat hair; you had to choose, and for me it was always an easy choice. For first time grownup meeting, I made an exception.

A black lady answered the door. She wore a pretty blue dress and her hair was pinned up in a beauty shop style. She looked like a TV mom. I gave her my new neighbor speech and she looked at me like she was trying to solve a puzzle. She seemed half friendly and half businesslike.

With a half smile, she said "Oh yes, we've seen you watching us. You looked like you were really making a study of us."

"I was!" I told her, excited, "Because you're the first black neighbors we've ever had!"

"Is that right," she said. Not like a question.

"Yeah, we've never had any black people live here, you're the very first ones. I'm so glad," I told her.

"You're glad?" she asked me.

"Oh yeah," I told her, "I'm really glad you live here."

The family's name was Walden and the parents were Tony and Inez. By the end of the day they and my parents were standing on the sidewalk in front of my parents' house and my parents smiled and the black man, Tony, smiled and the black lady, Inez, kind of smiled but kept her arms crossed in front of her and her smile was a tight thing.

She knows, I thought. I stood there, small, looking up at the four grownups, looking from one to the next and I thought, She knows we use that word. She knows we tell those kind of jokes.

I don't remember any of our neighbors ever speaking to Tony

I rememb
Ar
m

and Inez. Not that first day oi
were invisible. No one waved
hello when they were at the ma
door to door hawking his Boy Sc   ... skip
over the black people's house.

Every day I stopped by to say hello to Inez. Maybe she tolerated
me because I was someone to talk to. I noticed she wore dresses
every day, even when she was out working in her yard. She would
wear gardening gloves and sit, pulling weeds, in a dress, its full skirt
billowed out against the grass with her legs tucked underneath. I
didn't mention this to her but still, I wondered if this meant Inez was
doing it wrong or if other ladies like my mom were the ones doing it
wrong. Years later I would think: maybe she did that because she
knew everyone was watching her.

One day she asked me, in kind of a shy way, if the neighbor
ladies ever got together.

They did. In fact, they always met at the house right next door to
Inez's. I was sure she'd already seen ladies laughing together, going in
or coming out. My mom used to be part of that group but had
suddenly stopped getting invitations the day she and my father had
stood on the sidewalk with the new neighbors.

...ered my dad's advice, that I should try hard.

So I told Inez that yes, the ladies got together but that my ...n didn't go over there anymore because it was no fun. Inez asked what the ladies did and I told her the truth: they mostly drank drinks and complained about their husbands. I told her one of the ladies, Mrs. Carmichael, always drank a whole lot and would start crying and saying "I just can't stand it I just can't stand it" and then someone would have to help her walk home.

"My!" said Inez. And then slowly, "Well, I don't drink but still, I think it would be nice to sit and visit and maybe have a cup of coffee..." and with that hint placed, she went back to work, fussing with her flowers.

And that was how the next day my mom had Inez over for coffee. They sat in our living room and my mom tried to make small talk with her; the local stores, the new flowers she was putting in. My mother was a gifted talker. She could be on fire and you'd never know it because she'd be so good at talking and laughing in the right places; it was her skill. But it didn't seem to work with Inez. She always looked uncomfortable in our house, like she wanted to leave.

My dad did much better with Tony. Whereas Inez always seemed ready to be mad, Tony always seemed to be smiling or just about to smile. He smoked a pipe and the first time he came over he glanced at my dad's record collection and spotted Stevie Wonder's new album, Talking Book Album. "Mmm, Stevie Wonder!" said

Tony.

"Oh yeah!" said my dad, "that song, Superstition"

"Yeah!" said Tony.

I watched them both have the same reaction. Huge smiles, taking a beat without talking because that song was so good, there were no words to say. Tony looked at me and asked me if I liked that song and I told him I did because it just made me want to dance around all crazy.

He laughed, rocking back on his heels, and said "Me too."

They had three boys, all younger than me and a daughter named Kim who was a little bit older but still close enough in age for us to play. Kim and I, away from the grownups, would compare notes about being black and white and laughing about the differences. I learned that no matter how much of a suntan you got, you could never look black. No one would ever mistake us for sisters. That made Kim laugh. "You have to be born with this suntan!" she said, laughing. I told her she was really lucky. When she put on records and we danced around, she said I danced like a white person but that she'd help me to learn to dance like a black girl. I was thrilled.

We caused four near heart attacks at Christmastime when our family was over at their house and Kim and I announced we were going to dance for them. I told them I wasn't a very good dancer because I was white but that Kim had been helping me. Four grownups sat in silent shock, listening.

"Yeah," said Kim, "I've been helping Amie learn to dance like a black girl."

I helped explain, "Even though REALLY you need to be born black to have rhythm, that's just the way it is, that's why I'll never be able to really dance like a black girl."

"She's like a part black girl," explained Kim.

"Like light brown!" I said and Kim laughed and said "Yeah like light brown!" and we laughed our heads off and the four grownups sat, stunned, and smiled and said nothing.

For a few nervous months, we tried. But whenever I was over at their house, Inez would catch me studying her. I remember one time, in her kitchen, sitting at the table with Kim and watching Inez cut a sandwich in half.

"Amie you seem to be really studying me making this sandwich," Inez said. I didn't catch the angry tone of her voice.

"I am! That's the same way my mom makes a sandwich. The way you're cutting it in half, that's just how my mom does it," I explained happily.

And then I saw how mad she was. "Why wouldn't I make a sandwich the same way?" And she stood, a hand on one hip, waiting for my answer.

STARFISH ON THURSDAY

I remember the dad, Tony, came in the kitchen then and asked her what was wrong and she answered him in a rush: Amie here was just explaining how fascinating it is that I make a sandwich the same way her mother makes one. She looked at him with hurt eyes and I was all confused.

Tony put his arm around her and used a soft voice and told her, "She's a little girl, she's just learning. This is how she learns." And she looked back at him with her eyes unhappy. She told me it was time for me to go home.

It was often time for me to go home. One minute I would be at their house and everything would be OK and then it would be time for me to go home. I knew what that code meant, it meant I had been bad. And I never knew which thing I had done that was bad and knew I wasn't allowed to ask, only to try again to be good the next day.

And I did learn about black people, at least about this one black family. The same way most kids learn things: I watched, I listened. I learned that some husbands do nice things like put their arms around their wives or hold their hands or kiss them on the cheek; things I had never seen between my own parents. I watched with fascination on the day that two of the little brothers were fighting over a toy

Nixon mask and acting all crazy and Tony did not yell. I learned that sometimes when a kid was bad they didn't get hit. Sometimes the grownups just talked to them and explained things.

And suddenly, when one of my parents would make a comment about All Black People, I'd disagree with them. I'd correct them. When they'd say black people never worked, I'd say Tony's black and he works. And they'd say Well that's different. When they'd say black people weren't good to their kids I'd say Tony and Inez are really nice to their kids, I've seen them. And they'd say Well that's different.

In every category, they were different. They didn't do drugs, they weren't alcoholics, they weren't on welfare, they didn't beat their kids or each other, they didn't loot or riot or protest anything, they didn't seem to wish they were white, they didn't seem to hate whites. And they were black, which meant there were blacks who didn't do any of those things.

And we only knew one black family. Maybe there were lots of black people who didn't fit those things.

I knew I bothered Inez when I watched her too closely. What I couldn't explain was how happy it made me to see she was just like my mom, how every time I saw her do some little thing the same way, it felt like learning a mystery and the mystery was that they weren't different. It felt like an important thing to know; I didn't want to miss it.

I tried to figure out a way to tell her this but worried I'd say it wrong and then she'd guess my family was bad and then I couldn't go over there anymore and I'd never get to see how neat black people were. I liked them. I didn't want to lose them. I hoped they'd live across the street forever.

I learned a new word and it was Niggerlover. I'd heard Mr. Spears direct this toward my dad. It sounded like a bad word and a good word put together. I asked my dad about it. He glanced over at Mr. Spears' house and looked angry and then he looked across the street, at Tony and Inez's house, and his face softened.

"Maybe it's the right word," he said.

All of this, going into my mind's filing cabinet. Good things, bad things, parent things, kid things. I'd leave Tony and Inez's house and as I walked across the street I'd think, I'm going from the good house back to the bad one. I'd wish our family was more like theirs and then would feel disloyal, thinking these mean things about my parents.

My ears kept working and at my house, I kept hearing things. One night I overheard my parents discussing Tony and Inez, saying how much they liked them. It made me feel happy and I thought we were starting to be less bad. I thought maybe we were starting to be good.

And I remember the next day I went over to visit Inez as she knelt, weeding her flower garden, to share this information with her.

I told her our family really liked them. I said I had heard my parents saying so. "They said Tony and Inez are the nicest neighbors we've ever had," I told her.

And for the first time, Inez didn't look mad at me. She smiled a regular smile and looked happy and said "Really, did they say that?"

I was so glad I'd made her happy. So I told her more.

"Yes, they said of all the neighbors here, you're the nicest ones and that they like you so much, it doesn't even matter about the money."

She'd been reaching toward a pansy and her hand froze and she kept looking at the flower, not at me, when she asked me to tell her more about that.

"I don't really understand it," I told her, "but my parents said that because you live here, it makes our house worth less money."

"What else did they say," she prompted.

"They said the minute you moved in here it made all the houses in the neighborhood worth less money but that it was okay, that it was worth it, because you're the nicest neighbors we've ever had."

I was confused why she looked upset. My parents really did like them, they really had said that, and she had just looked happy only a minute before. I didn't understand why she looked so sad all of a sudden.

"Amie I think it's time for you to go home now," she said.

"Okay," I told her, and I shifted from one foot to the other and knew that something had gone wrong but I didn't know what.

"We really like you," I told her.

"That's nice Amie but it's time for you to go home," she said, her eyes still on the flowers, not looking at me.

So I went home and my mom was confused why I was back so quickly. I told her Inez had told me to go home. "I think I'm in trouble," I told my mom, "She didn't say so, but she looked mad, like I had done something bad."

My mom looked nervous. She told me to think hard and remember what I had said to her and I repeated for her the conversation about the houses and the money.

"Oh my God," said my mother. She said I wasn't in trouble. She said that was true, they had said that, and it wasn't my fault I had repeated it, that they hadn't told me not to.

I asked my mom if it was a bad thing, that she and my dad had said that. And she tried to explain it to me. She said the stuff about the money; that was true, so it wasn't like saying a lie. It was the truth and it wasn't anybody's fault that it was true, it just was. But that it would probably hurt Tony and Inez's feelings to know that, and so it was too bad their feelings were hurt, because we liked them.

I was confused. She was confused. She tried to explain how it was complicated, the whole business of white people and black people. She said some white people wouldn't pay as much for a house if there were black people living nearby and that it wasn't very nice, but that it was true.

In that time, in that place, it was.

I tried to understand. "Because they don't know how nice they are?"

And she agreed: "Right, because they don't know how nice they are."

I asked her if Tony and Inez knew about that, if they knew about the money stuff, about the houses and how much money things were worth. I remember what my mom told me. She said "They had probably heard that some white people thought that way but I think maybe they hoped that the white people here wouldn't be like that."

It felt really bad. My mom and I both felt bad and neither of us knew how to fix it.

And the next week, there was a For Sale sign in front of Tony and Inez's house. And a week later, they moved away.

That was in 1973. I waited, hoping maybe some other black families would move to our neighborhood. When I left for college, thirteen years later, I was still waiting. Our threeish mile neighborhood held only white people. Our city seemed to be only white faces.

By the time I'd started junior high school, I had a few black classmates, and I had a few more in high school, and that was nice. And they were nice. And every time they were nice I'd feel a pang of hurt, thinking how I'd missed out.

2%, that's how many black students were in my high school graduating class, a figure that would amaze my son years later.

He never heard those kind of jokes and was taught that racial slurs were bad words, that in our house, a racial slur would have been worse than the F word. There was no confusion. He was raised in Seattle and had diversity everywhere: in his neighborhood, in his schools, at the bank, at the store. And this was on purpose. This was so my son wouldn't miss out.

And when I sat, proudly, at my son's high school graduation, I stood, with the rest of the crowd, for the National Anthem. And when it was done, the crowd was asked to remain standing for the Black National Anthem, *Lift Every Voice*.

It caught me by surprise. And a young black boy stood, nervously, singing the anthem, first hesitantly and then with his voice soaring through the crowd, and voices in that crowd joined in, and cried out. And as I stood, listening, feeling guilty that I didn't know the words, I wondered why all high schools didn't include this anthem at their graduations. Why my own high school had not included it. And I thought, my son has gotten more, and I was glad.

In 2007 he sat on the couch beside me, flipping through my high school yearbooks. His first comment ("Where are the black kids?") was followed by my son focused, searching, evaluating. He wasn't distracted by the photos of smiling sports teams or girls in fancy dresses. He was counting. Black faces, brown faces, white faces. Then he flipped to the faculty pages, and he looked up at me, bewildered.

"There were no black teachers?" he asked. Politely demanded, that would be more accurate.

"None," I told him. "I didn't have a black teacher until I was in college."

"And look at this," he continued, his finger stabbing the page, "Not a single black administrator? Not a black principal or vice principal?"

I shook my head. No. Not in all three years. No, also not a Hispanic one. No, not an Asian one. Yes, all of them were white.

My son kept counting. He noted two Hispanic teachers and that one of them was a Spanish teacher. He found one Asian teacher. "And look at this," he said, "one black employee, ONE, and she was a secretary." He paused, to let that sink in.

I let it sink in.

He asked (politely demanded) to know why my school had not tried to get black teachers and black administrators. I told him maybe no black people had applied for those jobs. Maybe only white people had applied, so what were they supposed to do?

"They should have bent over backwards to get them," he said.

I told him maybe black people would have found that offensive. To be hired for their blackness.

And he said that didn't matter. "They should have done that not because THEY needed it, but because YOU needed it. All of you white students, and the black ones too. Because kids learn what they see. And what all of you learned was that white people are the teachers and the administrators and black people are secretaries."

And he was right. Kind of. And I told him maybe black people shouldn't have to walk around being lessons for ignorant white kids. I told him about Tony and Inez. Enlightening for me, not so great for them. I felt defensive, all of a sudden. I felt picked on. But my son had been raised to like the truth, to prefer the truth to a lie. We had done that on purpose.

He found a page in the yearbook showing photos from Black

History Month, with the two students who had created the photo display. And I read in the caption beneath the photo that one of the girls said someday she hoped there'd be a Black Student Union at the high school.

Someday. She hoped. She had made this comment in 1985. Apparently after having made this request of the administration (the white administration) and having the idea turned down. Because the idea of a Black Student Union for the fewer than 20 black students in a school of 1500 didn't seem to be reasonable. I got the math my son had taught me.

Someday. She hoped. I felt sick.

"Why would they have told her No?" I asked aloud. Not so much to my son, who wouldn't know, but just out loud, to the universe. Why would they have told her No?

And we sat there, a couple of white people who would never know firsthand what being black was like, not in our skin or in our bones or in our hearts. And we felt the confused weight of our color's bad history, resting on our shoulders, impossible to shrug off or even tear off. We wondered what the answer was. And we didn't know.

FOR YOU, FOR YOUR HEALTH

If I knew someone who told me they'd just won the lottery, my reaction would be: THAT'S GREAT! If someone told me they'd just gotten their dream job, I'd say: FANTASTIC! If they said they'd met the love of their life, I'd say: THAT'S WONDERFUL!

I wouldn't have to add: I mean for YOU. Because obviously the news is theirs: their lottery win, their job, their relationship. Of course it's great/fantastic/wonderful for them. This would be understood.

But if a person tells someone they've just quit smoking, what they hear for a response is usually: THAT'S GREAT! I mean, for YOU, for your HEALTH!

I'd heard people do this over and over and noticed they seem to all do it the same way. The THAT'S GREAT comes out immediately and usually is said just a little too enthusiastically. And then the person who just said that adds the next part in a rush: I mean, for YOU, for your HEALTH. And they say that second part with more emphasis than the THAT'S GREAT.

It wasn't until I became a nonsmoker that I understood. I was a rabid nonsmoker and then smoked for years and years and then I quit and it's been long enough that I'm almost an obnoxious nonsmoker again. I told myself not to be obnoxious about it but found the smell of smoke was pretty terrible. I found myself being irritated smokers were making me smell that—not when they were actually in the act of smoking, mind you, just carrying that smell around with them.

It's my opinion that when someone hears a person has quit smoking and they respond with the weirdly enthusiastic THAT'S GREAT what they're actually thinking is: THANK GOD I WON'T HAVE TO SMELL THAT ANYMORE. And it comes out with enthusiasm because they mean it that way.

But then they feel guilty. They remember, oh yeah, it's supposed to be good for the smoker to quit smoking, they actually get a benefit too, like not dying. And so they try to correct their first statement as fast as they can by adding: I mean, for YOU, for your HEALTH. They do this to correct themselves and I think they believe if they add it quickly enough the first person will not have had time to catch them being selfish.

SMOKING.

"His esophagus rotted out because of smoking!" They just heard SMOKING.

I think you're beginning to understand what I mean. Any other words you say in the sentence do not exist. In fact they probably couldn't repeat your sentence back to you if you paid them because now they can't think straight because all they can think of is smoking.

Do not praise them for quitting smoking. Do not say how proud you are of them because they aren't smoking. Don't tell them how much better they'll feel now that they aren't a smoker.

If you yourself successfully quit, the same rule applies. Do not play the Oh I Remember The Time game. Do not relive your smoking days or talk about the methods you used to quit smoking. If you must discuss quitting the habit, do so but don't use the words SMOKE, SMOKING or CIGARETTE. Do not torture the smoker.

Do not specify the times of day you yourself used to crave a cigarette because the smoker will be mentally agreeing with you and feeling cravings for each smoking time you mention. First thing in the morning (yes!), after a meal (yes!), while on the phone (yes!), with your coffee (yes!). When you do this you have taken one torture they are fighting and turned it into several. Stop talking. Keep those memories to yourself.

Because remember, you want them to quit for YOU. Be honest. If they get something out of it, that's great too but your first thought will be for yourself. You you you. Your nose, not their possible cancer. Because people are what they are.

In fact, when I was quitting smoking, the most discouraging thing was hearing former smokers admit they still craved cigarettes every day. Every single one of them said that. I had the 800 number of a Smoker Quit Line, designed to give encouragement to people trying to kick the habit. All of the Smoking Cessation Counselors were former smokers. I asked four different ones if they still craved smoking and all four said yes, that they craved it every day. All four of them had been successful smokers for over three years time. One had been a nonsmoker for seven years and he still craved cigarettes every single day. This was not helpful information for me. They sent a lot of pamphlets too and every one of them had either pictures of lit cigarettes or drawings of them.

Oh by the way, why oh why do some stores still STUPIDLY stock the smoking cessation products with the packs of cigarettes? This causes the person trying to quit smoking to stand, staring at perhaps 300 packs of cigarettes. If they need to wait in line they get to see and hear other people buying cigarettes. Some stores have figured out how to stock the nicotine patches and gum in a different area of the store: next to bandaids or hair gel. These stores have the right idea and the rest of them need to do the same.

Do I sound bitter? Oh yes. And it could be I have more to say, I can't really remember. I feel kind of dizzy and distracted because now I'm craving a cigarette.

THE GOOD SCHOOL

My high school was known for something terrible.

Oh, it was known for a lot of great things too; it was a very nice school in a good part of town, it was well staffed, and clean cut kids attended there.

In fact it was so nice it was easy to forget other kids went to schools that had less. I remember once I was showing two girls around who attended an inner city school and they were stunned, looking at the landscaping.

"Look at this," one said to the other.

"So your school, they pay someone to come and take care of these things, to water them and prune them."

"I guess so," I told her. I felt ashamed I'd never thought of this.

"This is nicer than any park we have in our whole town," said the first girl.

I hurried them inside, anxious to be away from the luxury I now felt bad about. But inside, it continued. They wanted to know, was this school brand new (no, 40 years old), did they just paint these lockers (no, I think they paint them once every 4 or 5 years), even my schoolbooks, which the girls took turns holding, turning the pages.

"These books are practically brand new. They have all the pages."

And the other: "Are ALL of your textbooks this new?"

Yes.

I got some perspective that day.

Nice school. Safe to park your car in the parking lot. Kids with enough money, or more accurately, from enough money that they could afford to walk around looking like clothing ads; could buy limitless cutesy extras. Through sheer luck of location this school happened to be in a district full of well-heeled people who consistently voted to pass school levies. Why not, they could more than afford to. And so the already great school got greater and the kids did even better on test scores, which made the good school get grants. So they could get more. More necessities and more extras.

After all, once you're used to extras they don't seem like extras; they seem like what should be expected, what you are entitled to. It becomes beyond you to imagine anything else.

Those other schools, the ones without enough books, with rusty benches and tracks full of mud too thick to run through, those schools seemed far away. Or more accurately, they weren't us. And so we really didn't spare a thought for them.

The kids weren't what we would have called Rich Rich, but they came from more than a comfortable amount of money. Kids got cars for their birthdays. One twin brother and sister received matching Z-28s for their birthdays, his with blue pinstriping, hers with red. Most of the kids had their own credit cards for their parents' accounts. Some kids had swimming pools in their backyards, some had tennis courts. A few had both. Our parents paid for salon haircuts and, before we knew the dangers of them, regular tanning appointments. Many of us took private lessons on the side for languages or painting or drama or dance.

You know, necessities like that.

And so the kids at this school had an easy time of it, with one very strange exception: our school had a lot of suicides. For some reason the kids who had so much often elected to say No to everything, to cancel out their futures altogether.

In fact our school had so many suicides, over so many years, that the state took notice. They brought in experts and did a 2.5 million dollar study to find out what the problem was.

For whatever reason, compared with high schools around the state, our school was off the charts in every suicide category; categories we came to know: for number of suicides attempted, for number of suicides completed, for likelihood the suicide would involve a violent (and more deadly) method, whether the student was male or female. And nobody knew why.

Those kids from other schools, the ones we would feel sorry for if we ever thought of them at all, had a much lower rate of suicide than we did. They lived in more dangerous areas, were coping with stressors we did not have and often with fewer resources, but they were better at staying alive.

The main finding of the study was that all of us had an increased risk of suicide before age 18 simply by the fact that we attended this school.

That was the only thing the study revealed. The kids who had attempted or completed suicides were from every demographic. No two were alike. The only thing all of the kids had in common was that they, like the rest of us, came from families with slightly higher incomes.

The money was killing us, it would seem.

How many suicides is a high number? I'm not sure. I know three months before I started attending this school, the student body president, an enormously well liked three sport athlete, drove his car the 40 minutes to Snoqualmie Falls, a scenic tree choked town built around its main attraction: a 268 foot natural waterfall. There is a restaurant at the top of the falls; it's a popular spot for pre-prom dinners. The student body president climbed over the safety rails, left a note anchored down with rocks, and then jumped to his death. Our school photocopied his suicide note and put it in the yearbook that spring, next to the photos of him and the words In Memory.

Not a suicide note, some said. It was a multistanza poem he had initialed at the bottom. The poem was about the importance of daring to follow your dream. Some (his close friends and family, mainly) insisted the poem was intended to encourage others to live. Other people said the poem sounded like he was explaining that his dream was to die.

268 feet to the jagged rocks at the bottom of the falls, and when they went to retrieve the body, they held out hope that maybe he was just injured, that maybe he had survived. In my hometown, kids are spoiled but they are also loved: a 24 story fall and they still hoped he might be okay.

Snoqualmie Falls was in June. In September, during the second week of classes, a senior girl shot herself. "Another one," people said. In January a junior asked the school librarian if she could borrow a pair of scissors and then proceeded to cut her wrists open with them, right in the middle of the library, in the middle of the day. She lived. We watched paramedics carry her out of the school on a stretcher and we thought, "another one."

Each time, the school brought in extra counselors. Often there were too many of them and they'd sit around the student center or walk up and down the hallways, watching the kids, available to talk. Anyone. Anything. We were frequently reminded they were there.

Teachers began asking the question "Are you OK" a lot. If you looked serious, if you were distracted. If you frowned over the grade at the top of your paper. Are you OK? Meant to be a nice question but instead always sounding ominous because it made you think: they're worried I might end up one of them. So then you'd give the teacher a deep look right back and assure them that you were okay.

We were instructed to listen closely to how our friends spoke. To take every casually uttered phrase seriously. To report everything, and right away.

This had the effect of changing how we spoke to each other. One minute you and a friend would be relaxed, joking around, and one of you would say something like "Oh God, I'd rather die than take that test again," and then you'd immediately correct yourself: "Of course I don't mean I'd REALLY rather die. I just mean I'd hate it." And the other kid would indicate that they knew, it was just a joke. No danger. Just joking around.

And then you'd almost feel guilty for joking around. Even though joking around would seem like something good for relieving stress and pressure, the things that might lead to trouble in the first place.

Tell tell tell. Have you ever noticed, the first five years of a kid's life he is told to stop being a tattletale. He's told to mind his own business. Then he hits age 12 or so and the same kid is told to report everything told to him in confidence. Nothing is sacred. He doesn't get to decide if the friend was joking or not, just tell and let the adults decide.

Telling is a dangerous business. And kids know it.

Because something every kid knows is that the kid world is separate from the adult world. Once you let adults have a piece of information they have the power to misuse it all over the place. They can ruin someone's world by overreacting. Kids know this. They know that kids might be just talking or threatening or joking. They might believe the small thing a kid is doing wrong will stay small and they'll grow out of it. Kids are closer to the kid truth; they often judge better. And once you report something, you can't undo that. The adults will run with it and you won't be able to take it back.

So there were a lot of kids thinking about the topic of suicide. We were being reminded of it several times a week by our teachers, by the counselors, by our parents. But we talked to each other. We made deals with each other. If you ever really meant it, you'd tell me. If you ever really felt like that, you'd call me.

I would. I swear. I promise. Me too.

The kind of deals only kids make and only kids keep. Why don't adults make these kind of deals? Even when they try, they seem to know the deal might not hold. The solid, I Promise, of kid world isn't there anymore.

Do we get weaker as we get older? Do things just matter less?

Junior year and the girl who told her best friend if she didn't get a date for Homecoming she was going to commit suicide. Reported. Intervention. Counseling. The girl despised her best friend for telling, scowled at everyone until graduation (note: is still alive today, thirty years later).

Senior year and the girl one year behind us who, one month after graduation, hung herself from the beams of her parents' garage. That was the same year our school was named one of the best high schools in the nation. We got a plaque from Ronald Reagan and, of course, more money.

And the first day of school in September, the extra counselors were there again. Scanning the crowds of kids, trying to somehow spot the ones at risk, the ones who might be next.

When I was in high school there was a popular movie called The Breakfast Club. In it, Ally Sheedy plays an outcast who comments "when you grow up, your heart dies." I think of those deals and how adults don't make them and I wonder if that line might not be true. If forgetting the secret code to being a friend isn't at least part of the heart forgetting how to work, growing cobwebby from lack of use.

Thirty years later, my old high school still maintains that sad record. They are still off the charts for suicide. It's still a nice school, rebuilt two years ago for no earthly reason except to spend the 85 million dollars it was given. The kids who attend there now can buy lattes from an espresso machine. They learn robotics from Microsoft engineers. They can buy truffles from the student store.

Danger from outside? They're ready. Armed police now patrol my old high school, one outside, one inside. There are security cameras everywhere. 'Non-specific drug sniffing police dogs' roam the hallways and investigate student cars whenever the administration feels like it. The kids don't have lockers anymore, just in case they felt like keeping anything bad in them. Or anything in them. The entire faculty takes Active Shooter training.

But the kids who might be at risk only to themselves, that's a problem they can't seem to solve. At that good school that seems to have everything.

STARFISH ON THURSDAY

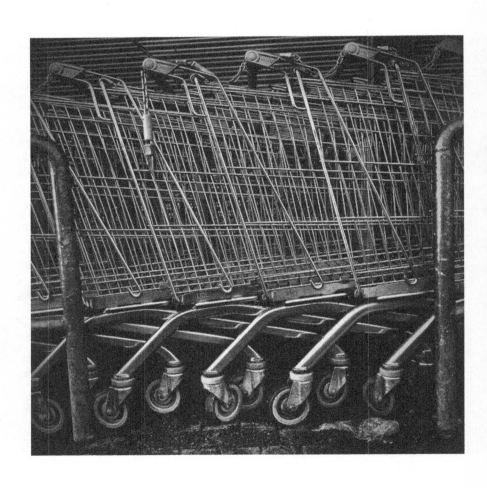

DEAR MR. ANDERSON

Dear Mr. Anderson,

My name is Jolene Markham and I'm a regular customer at your store. Why, I shop there every week (sometimes twice a week!) and for the most part, I think your store is just outstanding. As you know, in these difficult economic times, regular customers like me become very important. I've noticed your prices have gone up slightly in the past few years and it was somewhat disappointing to note your store only offers two kinds of pork rinds. Your sales fliers DO tell me I can get it all in one place and I just don't know if only two kinds of pork rinds really counts as having it all, so that's just a little suggestion, something you might be able to work on. No biggie.

My point being that regular customers are what make your business thrive. Why, it's practically like we're business partners, you and I. I spend money and your store makes money. Smart store managers like yourself know that this is just the plain truth.

Well Mr. Anderson, I just wanted to compliment you on the way you handled that situation last Wednesday, with the young mother and her two year old, you remember, the one in the pink dress who was just whining to beat the band.

I said to myself, Jolene, let's just see how this manager handles this situation.

I think I speak for many many shoppers here when I say I do not enjoy hearing the sounds of these spoiled children. No sir. The ones who claim to be "tired" and "hungry" and what have you. On some days it's all I can do to keep myself from reaching out and just slapping the spoil right off those little ones. In fact, there really ought to be a prize for people like myself who manage to hold back. Someday maybe there will be!

Well I watched and was delighted to see that young mother and how she shouted SHUT UP right into her little girl's face. I noticed the child quieted immediately. Mission accomplished! It was all I could do to keep from applauding. So many parents these days fail to correct their children properly. They don't get it that we're bigger for a reason and that reason is to be in charge. How else will these little ones grow up to know how to parent their own children otherwise?

When they spill their juice, when they do a little dance because they have to go to the bathroom, well that is a Code Red right there and that parent needs to be On It. In the middle of a store, heck, maybe in the very front door of the store! In line to see Santa? That works too. And if there are other people around, well good, let them see what excellent parenting looks like! Maybe you'll teach them a thing or two. Your child needs to have fear, yes, fear of you. It is essential. Having fear means your parents cared enough to raise you right, same as my Momma and Daddy raised me. Why on some days I could hardly sit down because I'd been raised so well, but that's what made me the decent person I am today.

Now, many store managers might have felt the need to step in then, to stick their nose where it doesn't belong, but not you. No sir, I watched to see what you would do and I was just as pleased as punch to see you do NOTHING AT ALL. More people need to take that approach. Smart managers like yourself understand that your customers could just as easily get their trail mix and beer and Little Debbie brownies somewhere else, somewhere where people let them parent their children as they see fit. And that's why it was such a pure pleasure to see you understood that, Mr. Anderson. That no matter what you might see a parent do in your store, it keeps the money coming in for you to just smile and say nothing except Have A Nice Day.

Sincerely,

Jolene Markham

STARFISH ON THURSDAY

AMIE RYAN

HEARTLESS

I've noticed a big difference between men and women. If you say something that makes a MAN angry, the man will remember THAT the thing was said. If you say something that makes a WOMAN angry, the woman will remember THAT the thing was said, HOW the thing was said, what the weather outside was like WHEN the thing was said and the shirt you were wearing AS you said it. In other words, women are terrifying.

This story takes place in the 1970s. At the center of this story is a guy named Jeff and midway through this tale you will feel the need to pause—and so will I—as we have a moment of silence to feel an enormous pity for the width and depth of the error he will make when speaking to a woman. Don't worry reader, we'll share that moment together.

Where was I? Oh yes, Jeff. When I first met him he still lived at home in a busy family with six kids, five boys and a girl, all between the ages of 15 and 23. They lived in a town called Kenmore, which is a very small town across the lake from Seattle.

People from Kenmore may correct me and tell me it's a city, and I would have to disagree. If the pharmacy sells penny candy, if you know the local cops by name because your parents went to school with theirs, if the hot spot of the entire city is a bowling alley and if everyone who lives there speaks in a vaguely Southern accent for no particular reason, that's not a city; that's a town.

Not much to do in Kenmore. The teenagers manage to fill their time the same way kids do everywhere: they try to get booze or pot or fool around, they fix up their cars and drive them, windows rolled down, radio blasting, up and down what passes for the town's main street, the one that goes past the bowling alley. They hope their cars look good. They hope they look good.

And a lot of them are in garage bands. In the Pacific Northwest kids love to play music, and they especially love to play the guitar. Most all teen musicians in the Northwest wear the same look: like they have all the time in the world and like they're glad to be alive. These groups make their own fliers to advertise and they plaster them up all over telephone poles, jockeying for space with all the other band fliers already there.

They play wherever they can get a gig. They play at house parties, weddings, reunions, senior centers and school dances. They take whatever amount the host can pay them and sometimes they play for free, just to be heard and just because they love playing. Sometimes these bands work for pizza.

And they work hard, these musicians. To be able to play anywhere and be able to take requests when audience members make them, they need to be able to play covers of the latest hit songs as well as hits, both fast and slow, from the music time machine. They need to know Blue Suede Shoes. They need to know Smoke Gets In Your Eyes. But more songs to learn just means more time to play and that's what these kids really like.

Naturally, they spend a lot of time dreaming about Making It Big. Why not? Every big band started off as a little one. And these kids of the Pacific Northwest, they hold onto that dream for a while, some longer than others. Some of them have the kind of parents who allow the kids to dream and learn how to like the sound of their children's music. They don't say Turn It Down, they say Let's Hear That One Again.

Because they know. They know the day will come when the kid

will join the regular workforce and that guitar will go into the closet. And when the kid takes it out to play a song he'll notice a layer of dust on that guitar and he'll feel a pang of loss that it is so. These parents do not know the expression I Told You So. Are there more of them in the Pacific Northwest? I suspect maybe there are.

Jeff and his younger brother Dennis were both guitar players. Their six kid home was a wonderful place to be. The front and back doors seemed to always be banging shut letting more people in and you could almost always hear Dennis' band practicing, either in the basement or right in the living room. Guitar strings, amps, extension cords, these were present in almost every room of that house. The parents knew all the band members by name and made them regular faces at the dinner table.

Jeff would sometimes join in and play alongside his brother for a while and then he'd get a sad look on his face. We all knew why.

I was quite young when we first became close to this family and my mother and Jeff's mother had taken me aside and warned me to never mention one particular musical group around Jeff. I knew the group they were talking about; I heard them on the radio almost every day. And then they told me the story I'm about to tell you, and then I understood why Jeff looked so sad, holding that guitar.

Jeff had been in a local band and he had had a good time for awhile, playing for low wages, sometimes playing for pizza. And the band he was in had something unusual: it was led by two girls; sisters.

The band used to spend a lot of time dreaming and Jeff dreamed right along with them, but only for awhile. Then he decided he was wasting his time and he decided to leave the group.

The sisters tried to get him to stay. They told him they were sure they were getting really close to a record deal. They told him if he left, they'd miss him. But Jeff knew better, at least he thought he did, and he told them they should face reality. He told them everybody knows you need to have a guy in charge of a rock and roll band, you can't have two girls in charge and that's why they were never going to make it.

Oh, said the sisters. Didn't know you felt that way.

And now we have our moment of silence, reader. Because you know this band. I'd bet good money you could recognize at least three, maybe four of their many hit singles from the opening chords alone. You could do that day, night, drunk or sober. The whole world was going to be hearing this band soon. A moment, as most of the men feel pity for Jeff and most of the women feel amusement.

Months later, they got their first record deal. Jeff called them, to try to get back into the band. The sisters reminded him they were still girls and that he had said girls can't be in charge. After that, they stopped taking his calls.

20 Top Forty singles, the cover of Rolling Stone, world tours, The Rock and Roll Hall of Fame. All without Jeff, but they managed anyway. People have loved this band for four decades. They play their slow songs at weddings, their fast ones usually in their cars, the windows rolled down, the volume cranked up, the listeners, more often than not, singing along, unable to help themselves.

I don't know if those sisters would like me repeating this story. Maybe they would. Maybe they'd say: You tell 'em, Amie. You tell 'em to watch what they say because someone might think he's dealing with a dog or butterfly when in fact he may be dealing with a barracuda.

AMIE RYAN

THE PERFECT ROBOT GIRLS

Actually this story is mainly about my friend Kyle. It also features a librarian, the downright mean and wretched lady librarian we had at our elementary school. I'd like to say something like: People like her should burn in hell, except she died recently and it would seem in bad taste. She lived to be 92, a good example of the kind of person who saves up their lifeforce, never wasting it on things like kindness, empathy, and feeling, and instead uses it to prolong their time on earth.

It's a shame I wasn't the one to write her obituary.

Why she chose to work at an elementary school in the first place is a mystery, since she disliked children. Or rather, she disliked most kids, any of them who might fidget or laugh or close a door loudly by accident. Untied shoes, strands of hair come loose from a braid, all of these things were repellent to her. She was only fond of the kids Kyle called The Perfect Robot Girls. I'll tell you more about them in a bit.

Back to Kyle.

We met when we were six. He was a pudgy first grader with a spill of dark curly hair but I was a small child so, to me, he was a big kid. One day the bell rang during recess, to call all the kids back in and he and I were left standing alone on the playground.

"You know, I could kill you if I wanted to. You see that green garbage dumpster over there? I could kill you and put you in there and nobody'd ever even find you," he told me, matter of factly.

I tried not to show I was scared. And anyway, I thought I knew the right answer. I told him "Nuh uh and anyway if you killed me, I'd TELL on you."

This made Kyle laugh and roll his eyes. "God, girls are so dumb. You'd be DEAD so how ya gonna TELL on me?"

I hadn't thought of that. I remembered the books I was holding.

"Do you see these books?" I asked him, "These are LIBRARY books and if you killed me and put me in there, the books would be

OVERDUE and you'd get in BIG trouble."

"Oh," he said, "Hmm well I hadn't thought about that. OK well then I won't kill you, today anyway. But I could if I wanted to."

And with that, he strolled back into the building.

Can you imagine if that happened today? A team of child psychiatrists would descend on my friend Kyle. But this was in 1974 so what happened was that night at dinner I told my mom I didn't want to go to school anymore because it was too scary. When she asked why, I repeated the conversation and this made my mother laugh. "Oh that cute little Kyle? He's not going to kill you. You have to go to school."

I kept waiting to hear if Kyle would threaten me again but I guess he thought once was enough. He turned out to be kind of nice and we became pals and after a while I no longer feared for my life. Then the teddy bear thing happened, sealing our friendship forever.

And I do mean forever. He and I went to school together from first grade all the way through to high school graduation. We're both in our forties, still friends; he's the father of four now.

Our class would go to the school library once a week and the librarian, the evil wicked one, would read us three stories. But there was much more to it than that.

We'd sit around in a circle, the kids on the floor and the librarian sitting in a chair and each week she'd begin storytime by reminding us of her rules. She had these three very fancy stuffed bears. They weren't toy bears like a kid would have; they were the very expensive kind that older ladies collect if they're kind of odd. Retail value of one of these bears, maybe $85. Each of them wore elaborate outfits, hats, and sometimes shoes and jewelry, all of the items dripping with cost. They were not bears to cuddle, they were bears to display, more like in a store window or an old lady's home.

She would remind us that while she read the first story she'd be watching us to find out who the best three kids were. And then she would let those three kids hold these bears all during the second and third stories.

She played this up with great dramatics, as if holding such a bear was the ultimate dream. She would then show us each of the bears and go into great detail about each one. "Look at the pearls on her dress," she would say. "Look at these shoes! That's real leather!" "Do you see how the folds of this gown hang just so?" And as she noted each detail we would sit, drooling over these impossibly wonderful bears.

And then, just when she had presented an enormous distraction, she would read the first story. I could never concentrate on what the story was about because all I could think of were those bears.

And I never got to hold one. Neither did Kyle. After the librarian read the first story she would go around the room and announce what each kid had done wrong to ding them so they weren't bearworthy. Kyle and I were both always dinged. He tended to make impulsive comments and I tended to wiggle around. Both things forbidden.

And each week the same three girls would get to hold the bears. You don't know these girls and yet, you kind of do. Imagine if you will the most boring classmates you had as a child. The kind that always sat still, that never said a peep; that were colorless bland imagination free kids with no real personality whatsoever. These types usually go on to student government. Kyle came up with the term Perfect Robot Girls and that made me laugh because it fit them so well. He and I both agreed it wasn't fair for the same three kids to get to hold the bears every time. The librarian could just take turns and then everyone could get to hold them at least once. And besides, those Perfect Robot Girls hadn't really accomplished anything by sitting quietly and perfectly still because that was the only way they ever acted, they were like that all the time and so it was no effort for them, whereas for active normal kids like Kyle and I it took real effort to try to be good. We tried very hard and they didn't have to try at all.

AMIE RYAN

So each week was the same. Kyle and I would begin with hope that maybe today was the day that at least one of us would get a bear. Then our hopes would be crushed and we'd look to each other with sympathy from across the sitting circle, and we'd feel sad all day. And the next week we'd try again. And each week the Perfect Robot Girls got the bears.

I would have been content to keep doing that indefinitely but Kyle had an idea. He told me this at recess one day after we'd both just been let down once again. He said we needed a plan. He said what we should do was to think really hard and remember all the things we'd been dinged for and try really hard not to do any of those things. And then we should think really hard about the things the Perfect Robot Girls did to make them so perfect and we should both try to do those same things.

I thought this was great, him making a plan for us.

And so for a week Kyle and I met every day at recess and reviewed all of these things and the next week, on library day, we were ready. We sat across the circle from each other, and he and I were perfectly behaved. We sat exactly still. We kept our hands folded in our laps. If something was funny we smiled but did not laugh out loud. We paid military level attention.

And when it was time for the librarian to give out the bears Kyle and I knew we'd been the best kids in the whole class. We waited. And we watched as she handed them, again, to the same three girls.

The Perfect Robot Girls.

And in fact, Kyle and I had been better than them. He and I exchanged confused looks and said nothing. But after storytime was over and we were free to walk around the library, picking out books, Kyle came up to me and said he couldn't understand it. "I was really good," he said, "and you were too, I saw you." He frowned. "This doesn't make sense."

And it was Kyle's idea to go over and ask the librarian about it. He said I should stand next to him and he'd do the talking.

She saw us coming and got a sour look on her face at the sight of us. Kyle said "Excuse me, Mrs. Thompson, Amie here and I were just thinking, we'd really like to get to hold one of those bears some week and today we both tried really hard to be good and we still didn't get to hold them. And we were kind of wondering why that was."

And then the librarian got a smirk on her face. Not a smile but a mean sideways smile. She put one hand on her hip and cocked her head slightly and I knew something bad was coming.

She said "Yes TODAY you two were very good. Yes you were. In fact, you were the best kids in the whole class. But you see those three girls? They're good EVERY DAY. They've BEEN good every day for the whole school year. So even if you and Amie were the best kids in the class every week for the rest of the year you STILL wouldn't be as good for as many days as those girls have been."

She paused and then added "That's why the two of you will NEVER get to hold one of MY bears. Ever."

And Kyle was speechless. And I was speechless. And we stood there, two silent children, absorbing this level of Mean.

She walked away and Kyle waited a beat and then he said "She just plays favorites then. Grownups do that all the time." And we shared a sad look that this was so.

All that night I mourned the loss of the dream of the bears. The glorious amazing bears, the bears beyond bears, the unthinkably wonderful bears I'd never have because I was a kid and didn't make any rules.

The next day at school Kyle came up to me and he didn't look sad anymore. He said "Amie I've been thinking about those bears."

"Yeah," I said sadly.

He said "I was thinking, I have my own teddy bear. And I'll bet you have a teddy bear too."

"I do," I said. I could tell Kyle was about to make this better.

He said "I get to hold my bear anytime I want to. I get to hold it when I'm good or when I'm bad or anytime at all. And no one else can hold my bear, just me. I don't even WANT to hold one of those fancy bears. Who wants those? And besides, they're probably covered with Perfect Robot Girl Germs and I don't want to catch those!"

"Me neither!" I agreed.

So Kyle said we never had to feel bad about those bears again. Because we had our own and they were way better. And then library day went back to being about books and not about feeling bad.

When Kyle read this librarian had died, he commented how much he'd liked hearing stories and I asked him if he remembered about the teddy bears.

"Teddy bears? What teddy bears?" he asked.

CLAIRE

A new girl came to my school when I was in the first grade. I think we all knew something was different about her right away because before she ever set foot in the school her parents came and spent a week sitting in folded chairs, observing our classroom routine. Our teacher acted overly humble and kind of awed whenever she had to speak to this couple. The third day they were there we were told we would no longer have painting time and instead would all go into the commons area and do vigorous exercising for a half hour. Pushups, jumping jacks, running in place.

Afterward, on my way back to the classroom, the observing parents stopped me and asked if I had enjoyed the exercises. They both wore huge idiot grins as if to encourage me to say Yes. I told them it was OK but that we used to do painting, which I really liked.

"So you mean you kids don't do this every day? When we asked your principal about it he said you kids do this three times a week," the woman said.

"No," I told her, "we just started this today."

"But you must have liked getting exercise?" she asked.

"Well yes," I told her, "but we already get exercise at recess. We all run around like crazy so I guess they thought that was enough exercise"

They asked me my name and then asked me why I thought the principal had lied to them. I said I didn't know but probably so they'd like us and would think we were a good enough school for their kid.

"Well don't other parents observe the routine before sending their children here?" the man asked.

This made me laugh. I said No, I'd never seen any parents do that before. I told them other parents just figured the school must be good enough, because it's a school. I asked them why they never brought their little girl with them. Why didn't she get to observe too, since she was the one who was going to be going there?

This made the parents exchange a look and then the lady said that was a good idea.

And so the next day their six year old daughter came with them, and she got her own folding chair. She sat, barely moving, for six hours, something I could have only done if my parents had tied me to the chair with rope.

At first glance, she made me think of Alice In Wonderland, except with something wrong. Her dark blonde hair hung straight and she had large blue eyes that were somehow full of doom. She seemed deadly serious for no reason and she kept her mouth closed in a tight straight line.

By the end of the week she was allowed to be in the class and her parents stayed home. The rest of us noticed she behaved strangely and she made grownups act strange too. We were told Claire had been tested and found to be a gifted child. Our principal and our teacher both seemed a little afraid of Claire, like they were worried they wouldn't live up to Claire's standards.

Judging from Claire's range of expressions which went from Serious to Bored and then back to Serious again, it seemed they were right. The nervousness of the grownups, the way they seemed so anxious to please her, it gave us the impression there was something of importance about this girl, that we were somehow lucky to have her among us.

She did not fidget or laugh, not in class and not at recess. Her voice never went up or down but always stayed in a kind of monotone and at the exact same volume. Efforts to involve Claire in games were met with her refusal and a dirty look. "I'd rather sit and read," she would say. And in her voice the message was clear: if we weren't stupid, we'd feel the same way.

No running around crazy for Claire.

The rest of us only knew terms like Smart and Dumb and we soon came to an understanding that when she would act peculiar it was like a symptom of this being gifted; not her fault and something she could not control, much like if she had a disease. The way the grownups acted strange around Claire, that seemed like a symptom Claire's giftedness made the grownups have.

My friend Peggy and I were working on being witches. We had read a wonderful series about girls our age who could do all kinds of magical things and this inspired many an afternoon with Peggy and I sitting on our mother's borrowed broomsticks, attempting to fly.

"I think I got at least one inch into the air!" we would exclaim. And we'd keep trying.

We practiced our cackling (two kinds: evil and delighted), drew sketches of our future witch outfits, complete with accessories of hats, shoes, capes and jewelry, and tried out different names we might use once we went witch full time. We both loved making potions and would steal items from our mother's kitchens: eggs, baking powder, anything that might not be missed, and would mix them in Mason jars. We hoped to someday be able to make potions to shrink people or possibly love potions. We wondered how we could trick a boy into drinking one. Sometimes these mixtures turned colors and sometimes we had to keep them out in the garage or hidden under our porches because they smelled really bad. THAT was how powerful they were.

We tried to involve Claire in the witch game. At first she was interested in the idea of reading a three book series but then read all three books in one afternoon and told us our games were silly.

"They are not silly," Peggy said, "They're fun."

But Claire disagreed. Whereas Peggy and I thought of books as a way to jumpstart our imaginations, Claire thought of a book as something to finish so that she could read another book.

We didn't dislike Claire. We just thought this being gifted business must not be such a great thing if it meant you never wanted to have fun.

We finished first grade and then second grade. And then in the third grade we all had to take standardized tests, using #2 pencils to fill in circles. None of us thought the tests were important but the adults must have thought they were. It turned out that three of us, me, Claire, and a boy named Jack, had all had high test scores and would be the three third graders from our school to go to the district offices for a week of further testing.

And that was how, a week later, we found ourselves with about 30 other kids our age, sitting at long tables in a classroom. There were many instructors, all of them almost disturbingly upbeat. We were told we'd get to use all kinds of materials and do all sorts of things. Puzzles, games, writing, and the most important thing was to be creative and have fun.

On one of the days I was given a microscope. Not a toy one, but a real one, just like in a doctor's office. I asked one of the instructors, What if I break it? And he laughed and said Oh you won't, just experiment and play with it. And so I knew these grownups lied a little bit. I knew microscopes were really expensive. But when was I going to get to use one again? And so I did what they said and had fun. No matter what we were doing in each class, the instructors stood off to one side, each one holding a clipboard, and they jotted down notes as they watched us.

At first this seemed strange, but we got used to it.

Each day for a week we spent three hours in this classroom and we had lunchtime and recess just like at regular school. The district office had a playground equipped with monkeybars and swings and a variety of play equipment. But they even made recess seem like a puzzle.

Each day we had to pick one of three things to do at recess. We could play a group game with other kids OR we could use a ball or a jumprope or a hula hoop by ourselves OR we could stay inside and read. Once we chose, we couldn't change our minds and the next day we'd get to choose again. "There's no wrong answer," they told us.

And this was a lie.

Jack chose playing with a ball one day and playing the group game four days. I chose the hula hoop one day and the other four days did the group game also. But Claire chose to sit inside reading all five of the days. I had noticed when they were explaining about the choices, Laura had looked fearful until she heard she could choose to sit inside. Then she relaxed right away.

During each recess the instructors continued to stand with clipboards, making notes.

And then the week was done. Jack's parents and mine knew each other and they came in together to find out how we had done and then take us home. The head instructor said she was glad they had come in together so she could talk to both sets of parents at the same time. It turned out Jack and I had scored exactly the same, and she said we'd both be welcome to join the program.

Jack and I were standing right next to our parents but noticed that as the instructor was explaining the details to them, she completely ignored us. She told them we'd go to a different school for three hours each school day and attend our regular school the rest of the day. We would do this for the rest of the year.

"We did notice one area of concern but it's nothing we haven't seen before and we feel confident we can correct it in Jack and Amie."

Both sets of parents looked worried, and waited to hear what the problem was.

The instructor told them that we hadn't actually been tested on any of the things we did in the classroom; they already knew we were gifted from our test scores. The only time the children were evaluated was at recess. She said that when given the choice to read inside or play with other kids, Jack and I had consistently chosen to play with other children and that we had both seemed to be genuinely enjoying ourselves as we played. "This was observed in both children, on numerous occasions," she added.

Both sets of parents waited to hear what the bad part was. The instructor said nothing more and to break the awkward silence, Jack's mother asked, "But that's good, right? That they like to play with the other kids?" and the other three parents nodded their agreement.

The instructor said the program required kids to spend a lot of time alone, inside. She said their research showed kids who enjoyed playing with others had a harder time adjusting to this. She asked our parents if they knew Claire. The parents said Yes.

"Well now Claire chose to stay inside every single day! But we can work with Amie and Jack and in time they won't feel the need to play with other kids. In time they won't even find those things fun at all. We can make them just like Claire."

And that was the very worst thing she could have said. This time it was my mother who piped up. "Yes, Claire, we know Claire. The child who brings a book to a skating party. We don't want our child to be like that."

Jack's mom nodded. "We like our son to play outside. It's good for kids to get fresh air, and good for them to be around other kids. We don't want to change that."

Both fathers were nodding but kept quiet, letting the women run the conversation.

"Why would you even want to change that?" my mother asked the instructor.

And the instructor couldn't answer that question, or maybe she decided she was wasting her time. She got a hard look in her eyes and it occurred to me that maybe she'd been a Claire and still was.

Jack's parents and mine decided, on the spot, that they wouldn't let us in any program that taught us fun was bad. We went back to our regular school, with our regular routine. And beginning the next week Claire was gone half of each day, but no one really missed her that much.

In fact Jack and I didn't see much of Claire until high school when the three of us had the same classes again. Jack continued to enjoy pretty much any sport that had a ball in it and I kept busy in pep activities.

And although all three of us went on to college, only Claire went to an Ivy League one. And she wasn't done. She went on to get her Master's and then her PhD and became a college professor, finally being allowed to do the job of teaching correctly.

And somewhere along the way, Claire married and had two kids. Her kids didn't need her to go ahead of time to observe any school routines because she refused to allow them to attend any school but homeschool until they were old enough to attend college.

I saw a photo of them once but found it difficult to figure out if they resembled her. The only feature I noticed, and then could not stop noticing, was that both children had her expression of Serious Doom in their eyes. As if they agreed with her that childhood was a serious business.

AMIE RYAN

AMIE RYAN

DIBS ON WHALES

Have you ever noticed, there don't seem to be any shark shows at Seaworld. I've never heard of a Seaworld show where they have trainers standing around on a shark's back as he circles his oversized fishbowl. I've never seen a Seaworld show where sharks jump up and grab fish from trainer's hands and I've certainly never seen a Seaworld trainer kiss the top of a shark's head.

Because all of those things would sound insane. You probably think this also, having seen the movie JAWS. Because sharks are dangerous predators. But what you may not know is that killer whales are much more dangerous predators than sharks.

In fact, I saw a great Youtube video last week. In it, a group of marine biologists and tourists were describing how they were on a whale watching boat, enjoying the sight of a killer whale and her baby when they saw a great white shark swimming right for the whales.

In layman's terms, the great white shark is the king shark, see earlier JAWS reference.

When the shark reached the whale, there was a great splashing and then both went underwater and the marine biologists and tourists waited to see what would happen. Seconds later the whale came to the surface with a dead great white shark in her mouth, seeming to be proud of her catch and showing it off.

"Like a cat would do with a mouse," one of the marine biologists explained.

You may have heard about several trainer deaths at Seaworld caused by a killer whale named Tilikum. (free plug here for the EXCELLENT documentary, Blackfish, by Gabriela Cowperthwaite, which specifically addresses the Seaworld attacks and gives the viewer a gorgeously up close look at these creatures, explaining why they do the things they do.)

As a matter of fact, Tilikum was one of many killer whales captured and taken, as a baby, from the Puget Sound in the 70s to be used in performance parks like Seaworld.

In the Pacific Northwest we have a group of killer whales who call our waters their home. I wouldn't say that we're used to them, because that would be the wrong word to ever use for a wild creature. We know them better. That's a good way to put it. So maybe because in this area we know killer whales a little better than Seaworld does, hearing about the whale attacks didn't completely surprise me because I've never understood why they don't attack the trainers at every single show.

Killer whales are meat eaters. They're predators. Their regular food is about the same size as a person; why would anyone expect them to be so sophisticated as to know the difference? No one would expect that of a shark.

And if you told someone, hey, it's ok, I have a surefire system here, between starving the sharks and keeping the sharks in cramped quarters, that's why it's safe to kiss them, people would think you were insane.

I think people in the Pacific Northwest have mixed feelings about whales being used in shows because we understand how cool it is to see them and we understand that not everyone has them swimming in their waters the way we do. Still, when seeing commercials for places like Seaworld, I think to us it just looks like a jail for whales, a place they're sentenced to for the crime of being amazing.

And so in Seattle we go about our lives, which often include boating and fishing, and have the privilege of seeing killer whales which call the Puget Sound their home turf. And we're aware it's their turf and that if we're in the water, we're visiting.

This is partly due to the fact that we have respect for them but it also has to do with that Knowing Them Better thing. We know that they're the size of a small fire truck and weigh thousands of pounds. We know that wild creatures act wild, not friendly or rude but just wild, and they could easily sink your boat, drowning everyone on board, and/or eat you once you were in the water.

So we show them respect and by respect I mean we kind of love them and are amazed by them and are properly a little afraid of them. They're seamonsters really, just real ones we're familiar with.

The specific whales that call our waters home are known as the L-Pod. Marine biologists here have been studying them for quite some time. They've tracked them, tagged them, and named each one. They know which are related to which, and how. Which are cousins and aunts and uncles. Perhaps they give them names to remind people of the Farm Livin' Rule: you do not name creatures scheduled for killing.

But they do more, and this is one of the reasons I like Seattle.

Advising the public about how to be good to the whales, that's their field, that's their job. Becoming attached to the whales, that's just charming.

Consider the following. The Seattle Aquarium had an idea to get kids thinking and caring about the killer whales. They held a contest, inviting local children to choose the names of each of the whales in the local pod. The Aquarium staff would then choose the best ones and announce them in a grand ceremony. Well! Thousands of Seattle children were delighted by this idea and sent in their entries. And at that ceremony, imagine the excitement of the children who learned their whale names had been chosen. They had named a whale!

And all of that excitement lasted until the Aquarium told the chief marine biologist what the names were. Remember, he had been studying them for years. He told the Aquarium staff the kids could call the whales whatever they wanted but that they already HAD names.

Translation: he was no Johnny Come Lately, HE'D been loving them for years. He was the one sending students in scuba gear down to the bottom of Lake Washington to collect whale dung, thank you very much, so it could be studied in his labs to be sure the whales were eating right. He loved them best and that was why he'd already named them.

Kind of awkward! I don't know how they explained this to the children. I hope someone had the common sense to use a term every child could understand; one that would cause no hard feelings: the marine biologist already had dibs on the whales.

STARFISH ON THURSDAY

Our whales, in fact, have been having a rough time of it. They were surrounded by food and yet suffering from malnutrition. Studies revealed the problem: noise from boat motors was interfering with their sonar, hurting their ability to locate fish and in general, bugging the whales.

The louder the boat motors, the closer they were to the whales and the longer amount of time the whales were exposed to them, the more the whales were affected.

The most powerful boat motors belonged to the state ferries but they weren't the problem: they ran on fixed paths, easy enough for the whales to get used to, and of course the ferries never made any effort to be near the whales.

Pleasure boats really weren't the problem. Because of the common sense thing, with the boaters being properly afraid of the enormous creatures.

The problem was with the whale watching boats. The larger vessels equipped with powerful motors that do nothing else except try to get as close to the whales as possible for the entertainment of tourists who pay good money for this thrill.

At first the Fish and Wildlife Department believed they could just give directions about keeping one hundred yards away from the whales, who were, after all, had been listed as an endangered species since 2005. They believed any boating captain would voluntarily follow those directions. This is called the Hippie Do Right Method and in my state that method often works quite well.

Pleasure boaters were already following this rule without needing any directive to do so. They understood that getting too close to the whales could result in said whales playfully and accidentally sinking their boats. And maybe biting off a few arms and legs to have as snacks. In fact, whales can swallow a toddler whole. Seals, dolphins, preschoolers, it's really all meat and it's all the same to the whales. So avoiding that was a strong incentive. And the people in kayaks and canoes, they were already keeping a respectful distance from whales for the same reason except a thousand times more so.

Commercial fishing boats were already avoiding the whales for the simple reason that the killer whales gleefully gobble up all the fish in any given area. If whales are approaching, give up, the day's fishing is done. If they're already there, forget it, there won't be any fish anywhere near them. To a fisherman, the killer whale is the competition they'll never beat.

But the whale watching boat captains didn't care for that rule. Up Close is their whole game. So most all of them ignored the Stay 100 yards away rule. In response, the state made the whale rules law. Unfortunately the fine for breaking the law and getting too close to the whales (starving them) was a $1,025 ticket—quite a deterrent to the average pleasure boater who already followed the rules and so, needed no deterrent—which meant nothing to the whale watching boats.

You see on an average whale watching trip they have 70 customers on board, each of whom has paid around $90. One outing brings in over $6000, more than enough for those captains to just deduct the price of the fine they'd receive and still make a nice profit.

In some places, this chain of events would surprise no one. Here in Washington, whale lovers were honestly shocked. By this time locals had gotten used to not only seeing the killer whales occasionally but trying to figure out, when they saw one, if it was Granny or Oreo or Deadhead. The Fish and Wildlife Department tried sending out workers in small boats who, armed with bullhorns, shouted commands to the offending whale watching boats: "You are violating state law. You need to stay 100 yards away from the killer whales." The captains of the whale watching boats ignored them and the tourists on board observed all of this and found it as interesting as the whales were. It was two shows in one.

So the state created what they called a Killer Whale Cop position. This confusingly named job involves one person trying to make sure all boats are following the killer whale rules. The person doing this job makes $150,000 per year. I do wonder how many social service agencies in the state of Washington could use $150,000 per year. I'm guessing all of them.

Oh but wait, there's more.

Amidst all of the news about the whales came another voice: that of the local Native American tribes. They claimed hunting and killing whales was part of their rich cultural history and one that they and their children were being denied. They understood that making the hunting of whales illegal was necessary because white men had been wasting them. The Native Americans maintained they shouldn't be punished for the wastefulness of white men.

And so our state court made a ruling somewhere in between. The state's Indian tribes could, as a combined group, hunt and kill one whale per year. Then the people of the tribe could have that cultural practice restored without damaging the state whale population. This decision was accepted by everyone.

So if you come to Seattle, I know you're going to want to see the whales. Who can blame you. But you can also visit our San Juan Islands and sit and have a picnic and just glance at the water and see them that way. I know, you want to see them up close. Bring binoculars. Or you could just hang out at the Pike Place Market and then watch that documentary Blackfish later.

Because if there was an unofficial Washington State motto it might be: We Ain't No Seaworld. And we don't want to be even slightly Seaworldlike. In this place you must be nice to whales or go home.

This story has been respectfully submitted to you on behalf of the Washington State killer whales:

Granny, Samish, Slick, Princess Angeline, Shachi, Oreo, Mike, Blackberry, Polaris, Tsuchi, , Doublestuf, Tahlequah, Alki, Hy'Shqa, Cookie, Mako, Suttles, Eclipse, Echo, Moby, Se-Yi'-Chn, Star, Notch, T'ilem I'nges, Sequim, Lea, Opus, Spock, Cappuccino, Sekiu, Scooter, Lobo, Deadhead, Tika, Cali, Sonata, Yoda, Rainshadow, Comet, Kelp, Satuma, Ripple, Spirit, Ocean Sun, Ophelia, Mega, Marina, Ino, Nugget, Racer, Kasatka, Nyssa, Moonlight, Mystery, Matia, Surprise!, Onyx, Skagit Solstice, Wave Walker, Ballena, Muncher, Crewser, Calypso, Nigel, Lapis, Fluke, Coho, Pooka, Takoda, Midnight, Cousteau, Mystic, Finn, Keta, Jade, and Joy.

AMIE RYAN

GOLF PRO

Some people still don't believe in Attention Deficit Disorder. I can tell you when I was growing up in the '70s, the boy who lived next door had A.D.D., they just didn't have a name for it yet.

Mostly what they said was a kid was "a handful" or "full of beans". Mark could rarely sit still and was most often nearly bouncing with energy. He was always somewhere on the Trouble spectrum— either just finishing his punishment, currently in trouble, or right about to be in brand new trouble. That was at home and at school.

It would have been handier for me to have a girl living next door but Mark and I played together anyway, from age 3 to age 7 when his family moved away. Because he was a boy, he would often insist on playing boy type games: football or catch or frog hunting. When I would try to suggest a game I'd like better, he'd say it was his game or he wouldn't play at all. And so I'd go along with it and try to find throwing a baseball back and forth fun. I'd play Lincoln Logs. I'd climb trees.

My mother used to say that someday Mark would be a handsome man and a few years ago I found out her prediction was correct. He found me on the Internet and sent me photos of him and his family. He has a wife now and three little boys, all of whom look like handfuls.

When I looked at the photo of Mark it crossed my mind that my mother had been right; he was a good looking guy. But the thing I noticed right away was the scar under his left eyebrow.

It wasn't a huge scar. You wouldn't notice it from across the room but if you were at a restaurant, sitting across a table from him, you'd see it. And let me just add, I know plenty of guys who would trade looks with Mark in a second.

But what I thought was: Oh no. Because I remembered the day I'd given him that scar.

It happened in the second grade. I'd taken baton twirling lessons and had gotten tired of it. And then I did what a lot of kids did in the 70s, I used my imagination and turned the toy into another toy. I remember specifically using it as a pretend old lady cane and for some reason finding it enormous fun to hobble around, hunched over, pretending to be 100 years old.

The baton itself was really just a hollow metal pipe and each end had a rubber stopper; a small one at one end and a larger bulb type one on the other. Naturally, during my old lady game, I'd hold on to the larger one which meant the small one scraped continuously against the sidewalk. Eventually that small rubber end came off altogether.

That's when most parents might have noticed it had become a dangerous toy. But mine didn't. And neither did Mark's. Both his mother and my mother saw us playing a game Mark called Golf Pro several times and neither mother told us the game looked dangerous. Neither one seemed worried we could get hurt. I don't know why this was the case and for the record, both mothers were stay at home moms with only one child home during the day so really, watching us was their only job.

The Golf Pro game was a perfect example of a game no little girl would invent but a boy would apparently find interesting. We would pretend that the baton was a golf club and take turns with one of us being a golfer, practicing our swing, and the other being a golf pro, giving us tips on how to improve our game.

The golfer held the pretend golf club by the end of the baton with the rubber bulb still on it, swinging the exposed metal pipe end. And one day when we were playing this game it was my turn to be the golfer and Mark was the pro and as usual, he was thrumming with energy and was observing my swing from many different angles and decided it would be best to stand directly behind me when I took my swing.

Yes, you know this story's about to get awful. I swung the baton back and suddenly Mark was screaming and running home. The baton had connected about an inch over his left eye and at the ER he needed many stitches. Our parents split the cost of the ER bill.

I remember I felt bad when it happened but that it had been an accident. That it could have just as easily been me getting hit as him. Mark had bandages over the stitches and over time, the stitches came out and then, before the scar could heal, Mark's mother left his dad and took Mark and his older brother and moved out of state.

And he moved back when he was about 16 but he and I attended different high schools. His family moved to a house one block away and mine had moved to a house three blocks away, so we never really saw each other except for the rare sighting and wave, car to car. I think I assumed the scar faded and then disappeared.

In any case, at age 42, looking at the photo and seeing the scar, I felt horrible. Even though it was an accident. I told myself it would have been worse if Mark had been a girl having a scar all those years.

Some guys think scars look cool. They make good stories. And he had played football; he probably had lots of scars.

But I still felt lousy. I decided I wouldn't mention it unless he did.

And he did mention it in his second message. He said he still had the scar from the day we'd been playing golf. He said he noticed this scar every single day when he looked in the mirror. He had told his wife it was his Amie Carbaugh scar and had then told her the story of the little girl who had given it to him. He sounded really mad.

I don't know if you've ever experienced this phenomenon: you do something that is some level of wrong and you feel sorry. And then if the other person blows it out of proportion, it actually makes you a little LESS sorry. And if they make a big enough issue out of it, eventually you decide they're an ass. That is what happened with Mark and I.

I sent him a message with a very sincere apology. I told him thank God it wasn't any closer to his eye. I told him even with the scar he was a good looking guy. And when I sent him this message I felt honestly very sorry this accident had happened.

But then he continued to chew me out. Same thing, he had had this scar all these years, my fault, et cetera.

And then I was still sorry but not quite as sorry as I had been.

But I sent him a message with an even larger apology and also a reminder that it had been an accident and I didn't understand why neither of our moms had stopped us from playing with such a dangerous thing, that I think most moms would have. And now, being a mother myself, the first thing I would think is my God, what if that had been one inch lower. I was really sorry that had happened, I told him.

Not good enough for Mark. Still angry.

And then me, a little bit less sorry and thinking to myself well if he hadn't been standing right behind me, if he hadn't been Mr. ADD case, the accident might NOT have happened so really it was kind of his fault too and besides, he has kids himself. He has to know this was an accident.

Then I felt guilty for being mad because now not only was I a scar causer, I was also a jerk. So I offered to pay for plastic surgery to remove the scar. Even though in my opinion (and probably in his wife's opinion) he was still a nice looking guy even with the half inch scar. If it bothered him every time he looked at it in the mirror, maybe getting it fixed was a good idea. A tiny voice inside me kept protesting that he and I could share the cost of the surgery together, even if I paid a higher percentage. It was an accident. I was seven. I told the voice to shut up and I offered to pay for everything. For the record, plastic surgery is not cheap and I don't have a lot of money, but I offered anyway.

No way, said Mark. And then he said the thing that made me totally stop feeling bad at all. He said he wouldn't let me pay for plastic surgery because THEN it would make the scar go away and THEN it would be like it had never happened and THEN I would feel better about it and he didn't want me to feel better. He wanted me to feel bad. That's why he wanted to keep the scar. Forever. So I would feel bad. Forever.

He said if I wanted to get in touch with him he'd be in Montana, sitting there with his scar which I had caused. I told him I'd be in Seattle and he could let me know if he changed his mind about the surgery. I NEVER WILL he told me and he also advised me my karma must SUCK really bad and that, just so I knew, if I got a headache or a traffic ticket, that was my karma. That is payback, and it is was what I deserve.

That was when he reached Ass level in my book. I decided to call it even. I had apologized. The END.

DEAR CANADA

Dear Canada,

Just writing to say I think you're great and to apologize for how very offensive we Americans are. Oh I know, you'd probably try to disagree with me, to make me feel better, because your country is so kind, so very polite, but it's okay, I know how it is.

It must be so embarrassing for you, to have a country full of loud, rude, gun toting people right below you. I've seen your citizens doing their shopping here, looking terrified, wondering if the wrong look or wrong syllable will get them shot. That's how friendly WE are, Canada, and it isn't very great.

Why, on our best day, when the planets are perfectly aligned, we still aren't as kind as you are. We are still Joe Pesci to your Cary Grant. Admit it, you're kind of wonderful. Tell a Canadian they need to wait two hours and they'll tell you that's okay, more time to enjoy the nice weather. Accidentally drop a piano on top of a Canadian and they'll say, Oh how kind of you, I love music. In comparison, if someone tries to say hello to an American many of them will just growl at you or maybe even say something snide about your mother.

On top of that, you've put up with our ridicule. All of the ABOOT jokes. Sorry. All of the EH jokes. Sorry. Teasing you that it's Maple LEAVES not LEAFS. We're sorry. Oh also the thing about the cops on horses, the Horsie Police. Sorry. Oh one last one, the teasing about the sport you do with sweeping ice with a broom. We're sorry.

Although how anyone ever associated a broom with ice, I don't know, but that's beside the point. Teasing isn't very nice and especially when you're so nice to us.

The thing is, you don't clean the ice with a broom. It's just confusing, that's all. And then when you add that heavy weighted thing you slide in the direction of the people sweeping....well it just seems like something you might think up while intoxicated. Not that you were.

And the money, your all different colored money that we associate with the board game Monopoly. Love that. Except the coins. You know, in America when we get a Canadian coin we can't use it anywhere. We have to give it to a cashier with the rest of our American coins and hope he won't notice and then we snicker because we've given him a useless piece of metal. Well, useless here, that is.

Oh and your holidays. You have a shocking amount of them, I don't know if you've noticed that. I suppose we do make a few jokes about The Queen Got Her Hair Cut Day. But of course we mean no harm.

Actually I think we all picture Canadians in some sort of parallel world where everything is simple and people have tea with moose. Either that or maybe they put vodka in the water supply.

Seriously, show me the grouchy Canadian. I will offer you ten dollars to do this because I know you can't. Michael J. Fox. He couldn't act angry if I set his house on fire and then stood on the sidewalk laughing about it. Martin Short. Please. He can't stop giggling. Anne Murray, she would bake me a pie. John Candy, when alive, would certainly have been happy to hand over his house, car, and wallet to anyone. I'm amazed he ever owned two pair of shoes.

That's another thing. Have you noticed that every time you have a talented citizen we steal them? We're greedy that way. Sorry.

It's nice to know we never fear you attacking us. You don't even seem to know how to insult us, so actually fighting us would seem pretty unlikely. Although I have to say I'm not sure how useful you'd be as allies, what with the horses and all. I guess it evens out.

What am I doing, it's not my place to tell your country how to do things! Oh, the Canadian Bacon, see, that's ham. It isn't bacon. It's ham.

I promise that was the last thing. Unless I think of more things, which I know won't offend you but will somehow delight you. Because they put vodka in the water or maybe because you're just that sweet.

Your pals to the south,

America

and P.S. If anyone ever picks on you, don't worry. You can count on us. We keep Arnold Schwarzenegger here, specifically to scare off our enemies. Actually that's not really him, that's a hologram. The real Arnold moved back to Austria about nine years ago. He couldn't take America anymore. Kept saying something about Too Scary Too Scary.

THE PAGEANTMONSTER

There are so many things I don't understand about child beauty contests. You've heard about them, I'm sure, and have maybe even seen some of the little 4 and 5 and 6 year olds who all kind of look like Joan Collins. I'm not going to lie to you; these children kind of scare me.

I don't understand what kind of mother needs a contest to find out if her baby is pretty or not. I thought all mothers found their kids to be the prettiest ones in the world. I'm pretty sure that's how it's supposed to go. But some mothers feel the need to find out for sure, and hopefully with a trophy they can look at any time they feel unsure about it.

And when these women enter their children into these contests they are truly competing with the other mothers. In my opinion every single one of these pageants should be called the My Kid Is Cuter Than Your Kid pageant, because that's really what the pageant mothers are saying.

Again, what kind of mother would say that to another mother: "My kid is cuter than your kid." In no corner of any culture would that be acceptable. Unless the women have a loophole like these pageants.

If the children involved just wore pretty dresses and walked out and twirled around and walked back offstage again, I'd still be against it. Because you're teaching your little girl that being pretty matters. A whole lot. And that if you lose it means You Weren't Pretty Enough. And you're certainly teaching her that looks matter because her looks obviously matter to YOU.

But these parents, already wrong, now go many steps further. So far that you aren't sure whether to laugh or make a face. I'm guessing they make you do both. These children, 4, 5, 6 years old wearing full faces of makeup. You think I mean they're wearing lipstick. Ha ha ha. Of course lipstick but also lipLINER. And yes foundation but also three different shades to highlight and lowlight. Duh. And of course 2-3 shades of blusher because you must CONTOUR THE CHEEKBONES OF A FOUR YEAR OLD or else she will not look like Joan Collins.

Bronzer, eyeshadow, eyeliner, false eyelashes. Well you need to wear false eyelashes because when the little children wear mascara it tends to run all down their faces when they lose and then cry. Not very pretty! No tears with false eyelashes though, and these little girls usually have two sets, one for daytime, extra long for evening. And when the little children smile onstage their teeth look perfect because they're wearing dental inserts so they look that way. No gap tooth smiles for them because looking like a normal child could cost you that trophy.

Wigs. And removable hairpieces. Message to child: your own hair is ugly. We need to pretend your hair is pretty.

Allover spray tans, artificial fingernails, support garments. For the people, mostly men, who have no idea what that means: it means girdles for four year olds. Some of these garments worn under the dresses not only suck in the childlike tummies, they also have padding for the chest area and rear. How these parents explain this to their children, I don't know, and don't want to know.

It does make me wish I could call each of the mothers and just offer to BUY them a trophy and offer to engrave anything they want on it, rather than have them put their children through this kind of warped experience. And there are a million of these pageants. It isn't just a once a year thing. They have numerous pageants and so many winners and so many trophies that I have to think the concept of winning would become confusing after awhile.

Even if your child wins, did they win a Good Contest? Was it one of the bigger pageants or one of the smaller ones? And just winning isn't good enough. The children are expected to be able to recite their Win Resumes: I got Miss this and Miss this and Miss this. They go year round. The child never has a season without one. There is never a time for the contest to be DONE so that the kid can relearn how to act normally and regain self esteem and maybe engage in regular childlike fun. Because you need to be training for the next pageant and the next.

Hey, maybe it's the child's fault for being born pretty. Or not pretty enough. Or the kind of pretty you need to put up to a vote from strangers. At least according to their mothers, the ones who you'd think would be hugging them after they've scraped their knees and instead are shouting at them from offstage and getting them fitted for high heels.

I don't know what the fathers of these little girls think when they need to take out a bank loan to cover the entry fees and the costs of the gowns and the talent coaches and the makeup artists. I imagine the fathers don't say a darn thing because they've learned the hard way, where the pageants are concerned, to let the mom be in charge.

The time they should have spoken up was right at the beginning, back when the Pageantmonster was small.

You see the monster isn't the child and isn't even the mother. It's the mental imbalance induced by the lure of the pageant and it infects the mother and the child. The monster triples in size the first time the little girl loses a pageant. The mother has little time to comfort her confused and crying child because she is busy being livid and plotting strategy for the next time. She is, perhaps, distracted, envisioning a Stephen King-like bucket of pig blood being spilled on the little girl who did win.

The pageant mothers invariably insist that THEY are not the ones encouraging the pageants; that the children themselves just beg and beg to be in them. I doubt that's true but even if it is, the mothers need to tell them no. They need to keep telling them no. And they need to explain to their daughters why they are saying no, in terms the child can understand.

Imagine, if you will, the different times in a child's life when he or she might be competing for something. Imagine the Spelling Bees and the Trying Out For Sports Teams, imagine anything where some kids win and some kids go home in tears because they didn't win. Kids feel those hurts deeply. And those are older children—10,12,15, who would have had time to have some kind of solid self-esteem prior to entering the contest. The kind old enough to have at least some perspective about how important the contest is in their lives.

So since your child already has all of those hurts to look forward to, why would you want them to have to start early and at an age too young to have any perspective? At an age when the child's self-esteem is an iffy thing? Not only are you risking NOT BUILDING a strong sense of self, empathy, perspective, you're actually DAMAGING their ability to ever have those things in full measure.

I wonder about those pageant children. After all, children can't really be blamed when they're raised with certain ideas and then those ideas come flying out of their mouths in day to day situations. Imagine the child whose closet is stocked with $500 hand sewn rhinestone covered dresses commenting to the classmate who came to school thinking she was wearing a pretty dress because it was blue and had a butterfly on it.

Imagine the pageant child who has been taught to avoid things like monkeybars because they can lead to serious things like scabs on knees and bruises on shins. Not very pretty! Imagine this child, somehow never really feeling like she's won, and all mixed up because she is surrounded by children who do not seem to understand the value of the superficial. Imagine her confusion when those simpleton children who act like children seem to be happy. That child must wonder: are they wrong or am I?

If little girls claim to wish for crowns, their mothers need to take them to a store like Toys R Us and go to the aisle where they sell toy tiaras and they need to show the kid how the store sells lots and lots of crowns, not just one. That's because every kid who wants one should get to be a princess. And that it's a dress up game, not a job title or an ambition. You don't need to earn it; I pay money and buy it because it's a toy.

And then later at home if the little girl wants to PLAY princess, go for it. Let her put on her five dollar pink fluffy boa, let her wear the plastic and rhinestone crown and let her put on her Cinderella strawberry flavored lip gloss that almost looks like her mother's lipstick. Inside the house, let her prance around for an hour or two and then have her put the stuff away because it's time to do something else.

AMIE RYAN

LOVE WON

Last year my home state, Washington, became one of the first U.S. States to recognize Marriage Equality. It was put up to a vote in a state election, alongside a measure to legalize marijuana. Of these two, the marijuana legalization seemed to have a better chance.

It wasn't because people in Washington were anti-gay or even against gay unions. The reason many voters were hesitant to vote yes was because our state already legalized what they called Domestic Unions for same gender couples that gave them all of the same legal rights as traditionally married ones. The thing a lot of voters had trouble with was the idea of same sex couples being allowed to use the M word of Marriage. To have their union and a traditional union being described with the same word.

I myself felt confused about it, and I wasn't really sure why. Even now I can't put into words the reason why I felt uneasy about it. But I can find the words to tell you what changed my mind.

They came from my old friend, Nate. I had known him since we were 12 and since high school Nate had come out as a gay man. He and his partner live in Texas and they've been together over 18 years. I admire Nate for many things but mostly for the way he is what they call a salt of the earth person. What kind means, what sincere means, Nate is those things. As an adult, he is that rarest of things: an honest politician. He works hard to make life better for the people he represents.

I was curious to hear his opinion about the upcoming election; about whether he thought the measure would pass. And Nate surprised me by saying he thought it would not pass. He said it was a big change. He said people need time to get used to change.

And then he said something that broke my heart into pieces.

He added, "I'm confident that within 50 years, we'll get that right." The right to use the word Marriage, the right to have their legal unions mean the same thing. My friend was 45 when he said that to me and I thought: **he hopes that by the time he's 95 he'll have the**

same rights that I was born with.

And suddenly I wasn't conflicted about the M word anymore.

I have another friend, Ann, and she lives in the Seattle area. She and her partner of 32 years were also waiting to see if the measure would pass. They are the adoptive parents of two beautiful little girls who would want me to add that they also have two dogs and five cats.

In the weeks leading up to the election, Ann and her family decorated her SUV with rainbow colored pom poms. Across the back of the SUV they had written: Just Married (We hope!) And on the side windows her daughters had used washable finger paint to write VOTE LOVE !!! and LET LOVE WIN!! They added lots of exclamation points and lots of hearts. Ann's family referred to the SUV as the Big Gay Car and Ann told her coworkers if Marriage Equality passed she was going to wear her wedding veil to work the day after the election.

Wherever they went in their SUV, people smiled at the words the little girls had written. They waved, they honked their horns in support. Wherever they went, people read the words and for a minute were thinking about love.

And then Marriage Equality passed. And our city administrator, Dow Constantine, opened up the marriage licensing office at midnight and his staff served champagne to the couples, lined up down the block, who had wanted to get their license as fast as they could, to say they had gotten it the first day. The couples waiting in line shared smiles and How We Met stories and sang several rounds of The Chapel Of Love. In that line were Ann and her fiancee.

And the next day she and her family changed the signs on the Big Gay Car. Written across the back of the SUV they wrote: Thank You Washington State Voters! And their daughters wrote LOVE WON !!! and again were generous with the hearts. And as promised, Ann wore her wedding veil to work, entering her office to thunderous applause.

And something I think Washington state voters realized, if not the day of the election then soon afterward. Marriage Equality was a victory for everyone, gays and straights alike. By voting for it, our state became better than it was before.

AMIE RYAN

GOOD ADVICE

When I was eight I started my own newspaper, *The Neighborhood News*. (*All the news that you should know*). I typed it, double spaced, remembering to XXXX out any errors, the way my dad said professional typists did. I used a three hole punch on the left side of each page and then bound the pages together with blue ribbon and sold this paper door to door for five cents.

Unfortunately, there wasn't much news to report: our kittens we were giving away, the ring I lost. I do recall looking in the dictionary for the correct spelling of *condolences* when one of our neighbors died of cancer. But then a young couple moved next door, the first unmarried couple to ever live in our neighborhood, and they became my next lead story: Living Together, What It Means And Is It Okay?

I had gone over and interviewed them at length and promised them a free copy of the finished issue which, by the way, sold way more than any I had written before. I began by letting my readers know that although we had all guessed by the shape of the new house that a 7-11 was going in, in fact it was a regular house. This was too bad, as we all agreed it would be great to be able to get slurpees whenever we wanted, especially on warm days. Then I told them the good news, all about the couple, Diane and Steve, who were not married and had no plans to ever marry but still lived just the same as if they were.

"This is also known as 'shacking up', although some people feel this term doesn't sound polite," I informed everyone who had spent five cents on my paper. "And just so you know, this arrangement is NOT illegal and Steve and Diane are very nice so you should be friendly to them even if you think they are doing something wrong."

It was a sold out issue but as soon as my mom read it, it was also my last.

I tried the newspaper biz again in junior high when I wrote a story about the basketball coach. He had described to me the first Christmas he had after his brother had been killed in Vietnam. He'd been traveling on a bus with a bunch of people who all spoke different languages, although none of them spoke English. He said they all started singing Christmas carols, the only English they knew, and that hearing all of those people singing around him made him feel the first warmth he had felt since losing his brother.

He gave me permission to use this in my story and of course I did but when I saw the finished version, I got my first lesson about the power of an editor. The teacher who ran the school paper had edited out any mention of Vietnam, or that he had a brother, or that the brother had died, since none of that was, as she put it, "upbeat". I told her she had reduced the story to a bunch of people singing on the bus, that she had taken everything of importance out of the story. And that if I'd known she was going to do that, I wouldn't have wanted the story printed at all.

I apologized to the coach, letting him know that taking out those details hadn't been my idea and that I knew his real story was a good one. "That's okay," he said, and looked crestfallen. I quit the paper that day.

High school and the school paper was fun and then in my freshman year of college I saw the movie Broadcast News and thought that Holly Hunter was just SO ME. Both of these things helped make my decision and I changed my major from English to Journalism. By my junior year I had done that one better and declared a double major in Journalism and Political Science.

I pictured myself as a wartime correspondent, running around dodging bullets while looking smashing in khaki and leaving men brokenhearted all over the globe. I wondered if perhaps I might snap an iconic photograph that would win a Pulitzer and be featured in Life magazine. Sort of like Meryl Streep PLAYING Holly Hunter playing me, if you see what I mean.

But I was disappointed to learn I'd have to become adept at computers, something I thought I'd never be able to do. I kept taking classes but with a sense of doom where excitement should have been. In one of my newswriting classes our final exam was to write a very descriptive story, and it was to be worth half our final grade.

The story I'd planned to write was about my friend Steve and his failed romance which he had turned into a great short story. I spent several weeks on this and had planned to quote extensively from his text throughout the piece. Four days before the assignment was due Steve told me he'd lost his copy, and I had no other choice but to find something else to write about, and as quickly as possible.

And so the story I turned in wasn't about my friend Steve at all but instead was about the day my mother hit a skateboarder with her car, and all of the chaos afterward. I called the story The Wet Street. I think I knew I was deviating from the news style a bit, that I hadn't really followed the directions, so I wasn't surprised when the chair of the Journalism department, who taught the class, had me meet him in his office.

"I liked this story. Of course, it wasn't exactly what I had assigned, but what the hell, it was great," he told me. He gave me an A-. Then he did something interesting. He leaned closer and looked me in the eyes and said "You know, this is the kind of thing you should be writing."

21 years later, I started taking his advice. Until that time I'd been waiting to come up with some wonderful work of fiction, some kind of story for the ages, and felt quite let down that I could never come up with anything. It took me 21 years to realize my own life was filled with a hundred moments of stories that were their own kind of interesting. My only job would be to notice them and then to try to tell them well.

AMIE RYAN

THE WET STREET

The original version of this story is long time lost. That's OK. I remember it well enough and maybe I can tell it better now.

Our neighborhood is designed like a maze. It has maybe 14 blocks of streets curving into other streets and to get to the main city streets you must first negotiate this maze, driving past blocks of houses with fresh paint and well-tended lawns.

When I was younger I used to ride my bike past these houses and as I'd pass them I'd think of the family in each one: The Smiths, with the daughter who went to school with my sister; The McNees, who fought in loud voices; The Dixons; The Normans; the Shiromas. And once I learned to drive, I found I did the same thing, by habit.

The day of the accident, it was spring, the weather warm. That's why the car windows were rolled down. I wasn't driving, thank God, but sitting in the passenger seat, next to my mom. And although my mother was well on her way to being crazy, and had days she spent full time there, back then she still had good days, days when she'd just be a mom, the kind that could laugh at a joke and sing along with a song on the radio. I loved those days. And on those days I'd pay special attention to every detail because I knew those days were rare; they would need to last, in memory, to replay as a kind of self-defense to try to make up for all of her bad ones.

And something else about my mother: she was a strangely good driver. Not just sometimes but all the time. All the little things you're supposed to do: checking the rearview mirror every 60 seconds, scanning from right to left in front of the car, maintaining the exact speed limit always and whenever, letting nothing distract you. She did all of those things and was the only driver I'd ever seen who did.

And when something unexpected would come up, when another driver would present a hazard, my mother's reaction was immediate and cool headed. No panic for her. No hysteria that could make a situation worse. My mother was the best driver I knew. That's what I told the police afterward.

And so it was a good thing she was the one driving that day. If I had been the one behind the wheel, I would have been driving at least 10 miles over the speed limit, I would have been fiddling with the car radio or digging, with one hand, through my purse as I drove. I wouldn't have been scanning in front of the vehicle and wouldn't have seen the boy coming on the skateboard. If I had been driving, this story would have had a different ending.

She was having a good day, the day it happened. And as she drove through our maze of a neighborhood, and as I was noticing how I still seemed to think of each family as we passed their house, my mother was smiling and we were talking back and forth. About what, I don't remember, something ordinary. And as we turned onto the very steep downward hill that would end in the city main street, I asked my mother a question and that's when everything started happening.

The first thing was, she didn't answer. And I turned my head to look at her, wondering why she hadn't, and saw my mother's expression had changed. The smile was gone, her jaw was clenched, and she was grabbing the steering wheel hard, her fingers gone white, and she had her foot slamming the brake, and was slowly steering the car to the left side of the road.

It was a two lane road, and no other cars were coming on the other side. She could only swerve it to the left so far because on the other side of that lane was a steep embankment, maybe eight feet down.

And then I heard a sound I knew I'd heard before but couldn't quite identify. Wheels crunching on gravel. I turned my head to the right and that's when I saw the boy. He was sitting on a skateboard, whizzing down a hill to the right of us, coming down the center of the street at maybe 60 miles per hour.

All at once those things happened. My mother braking, the boy zooming toward us. And my mother had gotten the car down to maybe 5 mph when the boy was right in front of our car. And then there was a thick thud and that was the boy. I could say it sounded like the sound a butcher might make hitting a very large piece of frozen meat. It was like that. Every time I think of this story, I can hear the sound like it just happened. I can hear it as I type these words.

First everything happened quickly, like time had sped up somehow, and then it reversed and everything seemed to be in swimmy slow motion. Looking down, taking off my seat belt, looking at my mother, opening the car door and going to the front of the car, seeing a woman coming out onto her front porch and yelling "I'm calling 911", seeing something to my right that distracted me, the skateboard, snapped cleanly into two pieces.

I looked under the car, at the boy lying flatly beneath it, and yelled to my mother to back up the car. She looked back at me, through the windshield, and showed no reaction, her eyes vacant. I yelled it again and used my hands to do Back Up motions as I did and then something registered in her eyes and she backed up the car, off of the boy. He would still need skin grafts from the burns to his back, but not as many as he would have.

Then I went back to the car to check on my mom. She had her hands folded carefully in her lap and beneath her breath kept repeating, "I'm just going to sit here." She had tears running down her face and didn't seem to hear me when I spoke to her and I was frightened, wondering if she might stay stuck that way forever.

That's when the boy tried to stand up. We looked out of the front window and saw, first his hand, fingers splayed out like a starfish, and then he was struggling to stand and we saw his face, and his skin was a wrong color white and there were dark circles around both of his eyes. Shockface.

And then the woman who had yelled was back and took charge. She was an RN in the trauma unit at Harborview Medical Center; she was also the boy's mother. I followed her calm instructions and all around us ran a swarm of hysterical children between the ages of 8 and 10, the ones who had been skateboarding too.

Aid units came and took the boy to the hospital and the police arrived to interview witnesses and measure the skid marks made by my mother's tires. After a few hours, we were able to go home. The police told my mother repeatedly she had done everything right. She had done everything she could have done. But as they told her this she still had that slapped look and I wondered if something in her had broken that couldn't be fixed.

When we moved the car I saw the street all around it was wet. It looked like someone had just washed a car there and I realized: that's his blood.

For the next couple of days it stayed warm and no one thought to take a hose and wash down the street, to wash the blood away. I wanted them to. It kept looking like the accident had just happened. Or was still happening.

And then it rained. And the street was wet with only rain.

AMIE RYAN

ABOUT THE AUTHOR

Amie Ryan, originally from Seattle, attended Lake Washington High School and Western Washington University. She lives and writes in the Pacific Northwest. You can follow her on Twitter @AisforAmie and on her website, www.amieryan.com

STARFISH ON THURSDAY

AMIE RYAN

STARFISH ON THURSDAY

Made in the USA
Coppell, TX
07 October 2021